—THE SECRET LIVES OF—
TEDDY BEARS

MY BEAR

by Dorothy A. Rogers

I have a Teddy,
A very fine fellow,
With brown beady eyes,
And a coat golden yellow.

And up on his back,
Is a tiny wee ring,
You just lift it up,
And it pulls a long string.

Then from inside his tum,
Comes an awful loud growl,
If you were a babe,
Oh, I'm sure you would howl.

It gives me a scare,
If I'm standing just by,
Though I know he's quite tame,
And would not hurt a fly.

His tail is stumpy,
And does not wag at all,
Sometimes I ride him,
And often have a fall.

'Cos he won't have boys
On his back if they're fat,
He just tips them off,
On the nursery mat.

You know it's just fun,
For it's gen'lly the case,
He waits till it's soft,
Then he ducks down his face.

And over I go,
With a very big thump,
For fellows that's fat,
Always fall with a 'wump'.

And then he's so sorry,
With his nose on the floor,
He begs me to love him,
'Fore he moves any more.

He's a lov'ly bear,
A very fine fellow,
With brown beady eyes,
And a coat golden yellow.

─THE SECRET LIVES OF─
TEDDY

BEARS

Rosalie Upton

Angus&Robertson
An imprint of HarperCollins*Publishers*

CONTENTS

These Steiff bears belong
to Australian arctophile
David Worland and are known
as the Worland Bears

6

INTRODUCTION

The teddy bear, often described as the world's most popular toy, has been loved for almost 100 years. While toy bears on wheels, sometimes known as Bruins, were commonplace in the nursery, articulated teddy bears as we know them today were not born until 1902 when American President Theodore 'Teddy' Roosevelt was in Mississippi to settle a boundary dispute.

Between negotiations the President attended a hunting trip where he refused to shoot a defenceless bear cub. A political cartoonist captured the event by illustrating Roosevelt with the round-eyed bear cub which attracted worldwide attention. An enterprising toy maker, Morris Michtom of the Ideal Novelty and Toy Co., seized upon the idea and made some toy bears which he named 'Teddy's Bear'. They proved enormously successful and President Roosevelt quickly adopted the teddy bear as his mascot, using it to great effect during his electoral campaigns. In Germany, at the same time, Margarete Steiff was manufacturing a toy bear with jointed limbs. Steiff had been a successful toy company since the 1890s and the new Steiff teddy bears were exhibited at the Leipzig Toy Fair during 1903 where an American buyer ordered 3000. Today Steiff bears are highly prized by teddy bear collectors.

DESIGN AND CONSTRUCTION

The design of early teddy bears was based on that of real bears and so the first teddies had large heads with eyes of blown glass or boot-buttons. They had prominent, elongated snouts and often the fur around their muzzles would be shaved. Early bears had a hump on their back and featured long curved arms which enabled them to stand on all fours like real bears. They had large feet and felt paw pads. A newly developed fabric, mohair plush, was woven from the wool of Angora goats and the texture was similar to that of real fur. It was a durable fabric which enabled early teddy bears to be stuffed tightly with excelsior, a filling of wood-shavings.

Methods of jointing teddy bears at this early stage were experimental. Some early bears had their limbs attached to the body by string or wire which proved unsatisfactory. During 1905 Steiff

Toy bears on wheels were known as Bruins.

experimented with metal rods which passed through the bear's body and extended into the top of each limb. A few of these extremely rare bears, some with their original sealing wax noses intact, still exist.

Eventually successful jointing was achieved using heavy cardboard discs which were placed inside the body and each limb of the bear then secured by a metal cotter pin. This method is still used in modern day teddy bears.

In recent years there has been a dramatic increase in the number of teddy bear collectors and, as a result, the prices of old bears have soared. Teddy bears have immense appeal and are loved by young and old alike. Their timeless charm reminds us of childhood and many owners form strong emotional bonds with their teddy bear.

The bears chosen for this beautiful collection were much loved throughout their long years of service and the saying "every picture tells a story" is

Above: A happy baby with her first teddy bear (circa 1949)
Opposite Page: A Teddy Bears' Picnic (circa early 1900s)
Courtesy Buda historic home and garden, Castlemaine, Victoria
Left: A bear from the Rippon Lea collection

deserved, as many of these appealing old bears also have their own true stories to tell.

My idea to compile a portrait collection of charismatic old teddy bears was inspired by Forby, a bear you can read about on page 42. His immense charm provided the impetus and after completing his painting I conducted a bear hunt around prominent toy collections throughout the world to seek out further suitable characters. Personality was crucial and, to my delight, many of the old bears from public collections had details of their original owners and since privately-owned bears had usually remained with their original families I have, in some cases, been able to include photos of past owners.

HOW THE PAINTINGS WERE CREATED

I wanted to depict all the bears as accurately as possible so, after permission had been granted, bears that were residents in public collections were sketched from 'life'. My drawings more often than not were covered with notes and directional arrows pointing to various parts of the bear's anatomy to remind myself of shape, construction and colours and to ensure the final artwork would be accurate. I sketched bears from different angles to familiarise myself with their overall shape and many of these sketches have been included in the book.

Above: Christopher Robin Milne with the famous Winnie-the-Pooh
Right: These cute bears belong to Christian, the author's son

Where possible I also took photographs of the toy to assist with colour work when I returned home to Australia. It seemed no matter how many notes, sketches and photographs I took there was always a missed detail and letters passed back and forth on matters such as the stitch direction of a bear's nose.

Some of the most famous bears in the world were recorded in this way including the remarkable red Alfonzo, owned by the Russian royal family at the turn of the century, the wonderful Worland bear who dined with President Roosevelt during 1910 and some rare and beautiful toys from the amazing Steiff museum in Germany. Then on to New York where, arguably, the most famous bear of all time lives — Winnie-the-Pooh, the bear who inspired A.A. Milne's enchanting books of the 1920s. The infamous were not forgotten and Horatio from England, a bear with a curious reputation for supernatural happenings, has also been included.

Because not all bears wish to be famous there are some teddies who have no claim to fame other than to have been dearly loved by their owner for many years. These special bears, in many cases, actually found me. Often during the course of a casual conversation I would be given information about someone's cousin, friend or neighbour whose family owned a simply wonderful old bear and I was encouraged to contact them. Many of their tales are poignant, like Ted who crossed the seas with his family at the turn of the century, the abandoned Plummy, the long suffering Jessica who endured countless 'operations' and the ultimate survivors such as Ded Ted and Treasure — teddy bears who were discarded and by some miracle reprieved in their final hour.

Correspondence with original owners and their families has yielded many interesting details and numerous kind people have graciously loaned precious family photographs and memorabilia for presentation in this book. In some cases an element of detective work was necessary. It was exciting for example when a son of the Rogers family was finally located and shared a first hand account of his childhood recollections of the wheeled bear, together with an old photograph and an historic family poem.

All told, my research for *The Secret Lives of Teddy Bears* took three years, during which my family were exemplary — especially my husband who was often condemned to hours of boredom waiting outside toy museums. I have been charmed by each of these wonderful old bears who have been such stalwart companions. Many are now elderly and perhaps a little shabby, but teddy bears have a timeless appeal that few can resist.

Childhood toys are normally discarded as the years pass, but the strong emotional bond formed with a teddy bear usually ensures it stays with its owner, often stowed carefully away in a box or cupboard to await the arrival of the next generation. For the many who have loved a teddy bear, to even contemplate parting with their old childhood friend is unimaginable. However, a few generous owners donate their beloved bears to public collections for future generations to share and the following pages are made possible by owners who have done so.

—AGED BEAR—

Private Collection. Courtesy of the owner, Jan Edwards, Ballarat, Victoria, Australia.

AGED BEAR resembles a character from a Charles Dickens novel as he dozes away his retirement snuggled up in a velvet sleeping cap.

At one time Aged Bear held a prominent position in the Museum of Childhood at Maryborough in Victoria, Australia. Sadly, the collection had to be sold and the subsequent toy auction held in Melbourne, Victoria attracted toy collectors from far and wide. Jan Edwards, the owner of the museum, had always been especially fond of Aged Bear and due to his advanced years and condition she felt it unfair he should face the trauma of an auction. A fortunate Aged Bear was granted a reprieve and taken home to Jan's private collection.

Jan had discovered the old bear in a box full of household bits and pieces which had been left at the museum. Aged Bear was found at the very bottom of the box. He had no ears and his patchy grey fur was extremely dirty but, as the old bear peered up at her with sad trouser button eyes, Jan knew it would be impossible to discard him. She searched through her collection of Victorian clothes

and found the ideal accessory for the bear, an old Victorian sleeping cap of red velvet embellished with lavish embroidery and a long silk tassel to hang over one shoulder. It suited Aged Bear perfectly, covered up the missing ears and gave the old bear back his dignity.

As the Museum of Childhood is now closed, Aged Bear has retired gratefully from the public eye to catch up on some well-earned sleep.

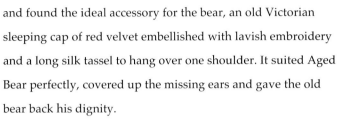

THE BEAR ESSENTIALS — AGED BEAR

DATE OF BIRTH:
1915

HEIGHT:
15 in or 37 cm

FUR TYPE:
Grey mohair, very worn

FILLING:
Excelsior/wood-wool

EYES AND EARS:
Original eyes missing, replaced with trouser buttons; ears missing

HEAD CHARACTERISTICS:
Wide head; prominent snout, with a few threads of original horizontal nose stitching

BODY CHARACTERISTICS:
An older-style teddy with long arms, curved at paws; all paw pads missing; bottom of feet stitched up with blue wool

DISTINGUISHING FEATURES:
Aged Bear is in a league of his own and unmistakable

—ALBERT—

Courtesy of Judy and John Sparrow, The Bear Museum, Petersfield, Hants, England.

ALBERT presently lives with Judy Sparrow's interesting collection of teddy bears at The Bear Museum in Petersfield, England. A very old teddy bear, Albert was made in 1906 and, even before his more recent adventures, was already quite a celebrity having appeared on television and in several children's books.

Life has not always been kind to Albert. He was rescued from a box of straw in a cold damp cellar where he had spent many sad years being attacked by malicious mice and moths. Albert's arms and legs were so badly chewed that he was really just a bag of bits and pieces when he was brought to Judy at her museum.

Judy is renowned for her remarkable skill in repairing old teddy bears and, with much work, she restored Albert to his former glory.

Child wearing a Little Lord Fauntleroy suit in the same style as Albert's

During the restoration, Judy discovered that Albert was one of the very early bears made by the famous Steiff toy company as he had a rare centre seam on his head and a metal button in his left ear — the Steiff trademark.

To protect Albert's fragile body against further damage, Judy made him a blue velvet Little Lord Fauntleroy suit complete with antique lace collar. This outfit covered the old bear's numerous patches and as Albert sat proudly in the museum wearing his flamboyant suit he enjoyed every minute of being famous.

In 1993 a burglary at The Bear Museum made poor Albert a victim yet again — being one of over 20 bears and dolls stolen. It was a devastating blow for Judy who was particularly upset by the loss of Albert. Reports of the theft were widely broadcast but only two of the stolen bears were recovered. Then, in late 1994, a sharp-eyed bear collector noticed a teddy who looked remarkably like Albert sitting in a London antique shop. Judy rushed to London from Petersfield and identified the bear as Albert the following morning.

Albert had survived his adventures reasonably well, although he had lost his beautiful suit and his eyes had been changed. No bear was happier to be home.

Albert intends to retire from public life for the time being — after his latest misadventure he considers the price of fame a little high!

THE BEAR ESSENTIALS — ALBERT

DATE OF BIRTH:
1906 Steiff bear made in Germany

HEIGHT:
16 in or 41 cm

FUR TYPE:
Originally gold coloured mohair, very worn condition

FILLING:
Excelsior/wood-wool

EYES AND EARS:
Black boot-button type, not original

HEAD CHARACTERISTICS:
Rare centre seam on head, used by Steiff to economise on expensive mohair fabric; long snout, nose stitched vertically, not original; metal button in left ear

BODY CHARACTERISTICS:
Humped back; very long arms with curved paws; paw pads repaired with pale green twill; very long feet

DISTINGUISHING FEATURES:
Distinctive centre seam on head which only one in every seven Steiff bears had at this time (1906), a method used by Steiff to avoid unnecessary wastage of expensive mohair fabric; very little fur remains on the bear and he is in fragile condition

―ALFONZO―

Public Collection. Courtesy of Ian Pout and the Teddy Bears of Witney Museum, Witney, Oxfordshire, England.

ALFONZO has a very regal air about him and he has every right to look imperious because he once belonged to the Russian Royal Family. Alfonzo is an exceptionally rare red Steiff teddy bear. He was given to Princess Xenia in 1908 when she was four years old by her father, George Michailovich, the Grand Duke of Russia. Princess Xenia was cousin and playmate to Princess Anastasia Romanov, the Czar's daughter, who was later executed with her family at Ekaterinburg during the Russian Revolution. Alfonzo was a favourite of the little princesses and his Cossack outfit of yellow satin is believed to have been made by Princess Xenia's English nanny, Miss Ball.

In 1914, 10 year old Princess Xenia and her mother travelled to London to visit their royal relatives at Buckingham Palace. Shortly after they arrived the First World War broke out, so mother and daughter took a house in Chester Square to avoid the danger of returning to Russia. Princess Xenia was never to see her father again. The Revolution swept through Russia during 1917 and in 1919 the Grand Duke Michailovich was assassinated in St Petersburg. Alfonzo was a treasured memento of her father and remained with Princess Xenia until her death in 1965.

In May 1989 Alfonzo was auctioned at Christie's in London and purchased by the Teddy Bears of Witney Museum in Witney, England, for what was then a world record price of £12,000. Due to the bear's remarkable history the museum had special replicas of Alfonzo made by Steiff, manufacturer of the original. To ensure accuracy, Alfonzo was flown to Germany where he was carefully copied right down to the last detail.

Alfonzo now has time to reflect on his illustrious past in the Russian Royal Court, as he reclines on his antique tapestry wrap, which was specially chosen to complement the colour of his extraordinary red fur.

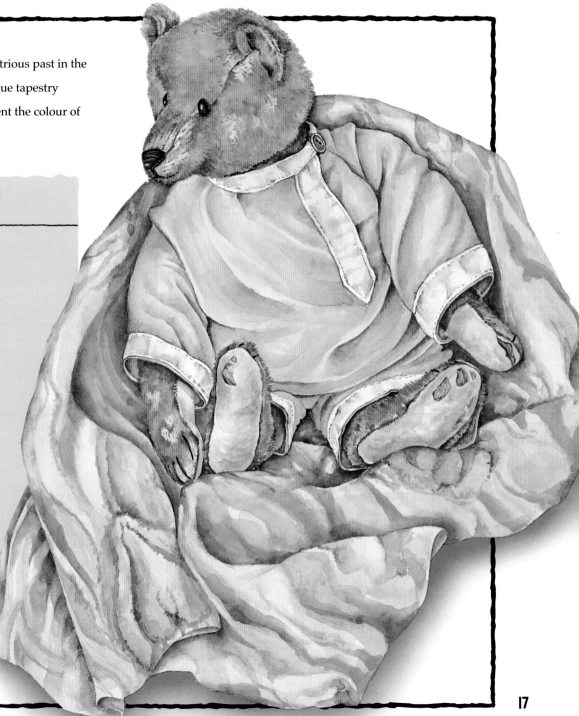

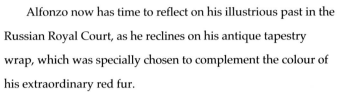

THE BEAR ESSENTIALS — ALFONZO

DATE OF BIRTH:
1908 Steiff bear made in Germany

HEIGHT:
13 in or 32 cm

FUR TYPE:
Rust-red mohair plush, slightly worn in places to reveal base of beige cloth

FILLING:
Excelsior/wood-wool

EYES AND EARS:
Black button eyes; ears set wide apart

HEAD CHARACTERISTICS:
Pronounced and quite pointed snout; black horizontal stitching on nose

BODY CHARACTERISTICS:
Long arms; paw pads original beige felt, four claws on each paw; large feet

DISTINGUISHING FEATURES:
Alfonzo's rare, unusual colour; original hand-sewn Cossack outfit, circa 1908

‑BEAR AND BATMAN'S DOLL‑

*Doll in Public Collection. Courtesy of the La Trobe Collection,
State Library of Victoria, Melbourne, Australia.
Bear in Private Collection. By courtesy of the owner.*

IN 1835 John Batman, one of the first white settlers in Melbourne, stood on the site which was to become the city and its suburbs and wrote in his diary "This will be the place for a village".

John Batman signed his controversial land treaty with the Aborigines and for blankets, tomahawks and knives he gained 600 acres of prime land.

The father of a large family, John Batman had eight children and the small doll pictured here belonged to his fourth daughter, Elizabeth. It is believed Batman purchased the doll while visiting England in the 1830s. The doll's hand-sewn clothes and red velvet bonnet are thought to be original. The Batman family arrived at the new settlement in Melbourne in 1836, when Elizabeth was seven years old. As one of the first white children in the area the little girl had few friends and the doll became her treasured childhood companion.

Later, Elizabeth married and the precious doll was passed down through her family. For a long time the family regarded the doll as having personal, not historical, value and throughout the period of two World Wars the doll was often displayed at Red Cross and patriotic functions to boost funds. The doll was later donated to the La Trobe Collection, State Library of Victoria by Miss Alison Searle, the great-great-granddaughter of John Batman.

The old bear pictured holding the doll was seen in an antiquarian book shop sitting on a pile of dusty newspapers with a history book. The owner of the shop said the bear had been there for as long as he could recall — it had belonged to his uncle, the original owner of the shop. The uncle had been a distinguished, if rather unconventional, academic who had lectured at prominent universities around the world and had always taken the bear with him. When he retired and opened the book shop his bear came too and, over the years, due to constant exposure to old, musty books most of the bear's fur had been nibbled away by silverfish. To his customers' amusement he would often hold lengthy one-sided conversations with the bear about the weather, politics or any other subject which took his fancy.

The uncle's name was also John and so, with some artistic licence, there seemed no better companion for the Batman doll than this educated, well travelled bear with a passion for history.

THE DOLL ESSENTIALS — THE BATMAN DOLL

DATE OF BIRTH:
Circa 1830s

HEIGHT:
9 in or 22.5 cm

BODY CHARACTERISTICS:
A stuffed cloth body with kid leather arms

HEAD CHARACTERISTICS:
A painted china face

COSTUME:
Skirt is pintucked around the hem, she wears a pinafore of white linen, shoes are of red cloth and there is a matching red bonnet

DISTINGUISHING FEATURES:
Inside the hem of the doll's skirt is the name 'Searle' handwritten in black ink

THE BEAR ESSENTIALS — BEAR

DATE OF BIRTH:
Circa 1910 probably made in Germany, characteristic of Gebruder Bing

HEIGHT:
23 in or 57 cm

FUR TYPE:
Pale golden mohair, very worn condition

FILLING:
Excelsior/wood wool

EYES AND EARS:
Original flat boot-button type eyes; large cup-shaped ears set low on side of head

HEAD CHARACTERISTICS:
Broad head with ears positioned well to side of head; clipped muzzle; black silk nose, stitched vertically

BODY CHARACTERISTICS:
Large hump on back; long limbs and very large feet; four original claws on each paw

DISTINGUISHING FEATURES:
All the bear's paw pads have been repaired with faded pink upholstery fabric; body fabric extremely fragile due to infestation by silverfish, patches above left eye and on front of body

–BILL BEAR–

Private Collection. Courtesy of the owner, Kent, England.

THE INTREPID Bill Bear survived many adventures in his younger days and even attended boarding school, until his education was cut short by a flying accident.

Bill Bear accompanied five year old Peter to boarding school during the early 1950s. Peter regarded Bill as his best friend and ignored the schoolboy taunts and raised eyebrows as he unpacked Bill from his suitcase on their first night away from home. Unfortunately boarding school life soon took a turn for the worse and one night some naughty boys in the dormitory kidnapped Bill for a parachute jump. In spite of Peter's fervent pleas poor old Bill was attached to a large handkerchief and launched from a third floor window. After an extensive search in the dark by angry teachers, tired students and a very distraught Peter, Bill Bear was found stuck high in a tree. At this point the Housemaster advised Peter that a bear may not be suited to an education and, the following day, Bill Bear was mailed home to Kent in a large biscuit tin.

Peter's mother was surprised but very pleased to see the old bear, packed tightly in his biscuit tin, together with a letter of explanation from Peter. Bill was still wearing his striped pyjamas and had lost an eye but looked none the worse for his adventure. Peter's mother wrapped him up in an old cot blanket with a handful of moth balls and stored him carefully away in the back of a cupboard.

Many years later, when he was married with three sons of his own, Peter suddenly remembered his old bear and asked his mother if she could find him. The cupboards were searched and Bill Bear emerged gratefully from his wool baby blanket and is currently caring for a new generation of small boys.

THE BEAR ESSENTIALS — BILL BEAR

DATE OF BIRTH:
Circa 1940

HEIGHT:
15 in or 37 cm

FUR TYPE:
Golden coloured mohair, worn condition

FILLING:
Excelsior/wood-wool and kapok

EYES AND EARS:
One original glass eye; small ears set below side seam and inserted into head

HEAD CHARACTERISTICS:
Short muzzle, nose restitched; mouth missing

BODY CHARACTERISTICS:
Round body; short thin arms with original rexine pads; shaped legs, no claws

DISTINGUISHING FEATURES:
One eye missing; Bill has worn pyjama trousers for most of his life and subsequently his legs have more fur than the rest of his body

—BRIDAL BEARS—

Public Collection. Courtesy of the Spielzeugmuseum im Alten Rathausturm, Munich, Germany.

MUNICH, the capital of Bavaria, is home to the Spielzeugmuseum which is situated in an historic tower close to the old city gates. The collection contains many interesting examples of early German toys.

A narrow spiral staircase winds up through the old stone building and each floor opens to a room full of toys. One or two precious items date from the Renaissance era, however most of the toys date from the 19th century. The teddy bear collection is situated on the upper floor and as Steiff, the famous manufacturer of teddy bears, is a German company it is not surprising that many of the magnificent bears on display are in fact Steiff bears, which were made at the turn of the century.

Due to the ever increasing popularity of teddy bears, the collection is in constant demand from photographers. On the day the Bridal Bears were recorded many of their companions were out on location doing a shoot for some forthcoming Christmas cards, so the happy couple were quietly tucked away together in a corner of the museum. The groom was wearing a dark suit with matching woollen socks and held a Bavarian hat on his lap. His bride stood alongside wearing a headdress trimmed with silk flowers and a long antique silk veil which trailed gracefully after her.

With their stern expressions, reminiscent of old Victorian wedding portraits, the couple would have been completely at home in any bridal party.

THE BEAR ESSENTIALS —

THE GROOM

DATE OF BIRTH:
Circa 1915 probably made in Germany

FUR TYPE:
White mohair plush

FILLING:
Excelsior/wood wool

EYES AND EARS:
Amber glass eyes; rounded ears set high on his head

BODY CHARACTERISTICS:
Has tan silk claws and original felt paw pads

DISTINGUISHING FEATURES:
Wears a handmade suit of woollen cloth,
fastened with white buttons, also wears
matching socks and a Bavarian-style hat

THE BRIDE

DATE OF BIRTH:
Circa early 1900s made in Germany,
possibly by Steiff

FUR TYPE:
White mohair in excellent condition

FILLING:
Excelsior/wood wool

EYES AND EARS:
Original boot-button eyes

HEAD CHARACTERISTICS:
Pronounced shaved muzzle;
vertically stitched nose in tan silk

BODY CHARACTERISTICS:
Humped back, long limbs with original felt paw pads

DISTINGUISHING FEATURES:
Made from rare and desirable white mohair,
the bear wears an antique baby's dress
and an antique bridal headdress

23

—CATTLEY FAMILY TOYS—

By courtesy of the Board of Trustees of the Victoria and Albert Museum, London, England.

THE LITTLE characters on these pages are just a handful from a collection of 15 delightful toys which all belonged to the Cattley family at the turn of the century. The toys were made in Germany circa 1906 and are particularly interesting as they represent early examples of small, mass-produced toys.

The four Cattley children, Maud Evelyn, Constance Emily, Helen Edith and Gilbert Acheson, were born between 1885 and 1892. Their toys were very special to the children and each was given a name. The bear in the white dress on the left of the group (opposite page) was called Baby Georgie whilst the velveteen rabbit was known simply as Ben. Their exquisite clothes were hand-sewn by the children and their mother, Edith Louise. Each toy was fortunate enough to have several different outfits.

When the Cattleys left home for their annual trip to the seaside this menagerie of soft toys accompanied them. At the seaside the children would take photographs of their toys posed on the beach and later compiled a photograph album of these shots. The Cattley children and

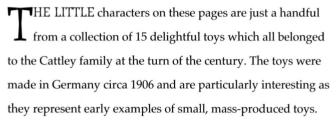

Just three of the wonderful Cattley Family Toys – some were given names – "Baby Georgie" in a white lace dress – "Ben the rabbit. All the toys wear beautiful handsewn clothes made by the Cattley children in the early 1900's. All the toys and shop outfits, photographs and their own paintings are at the Bethnal Green Museum, London, U.K.

their mother were also talented artists and created an album containing 23 watercolour paintings of the toys. Both these albums can be seen at the Bethnal Green Museum of

the Cattley family toys.

Childhood where the Cattley toys and their extensive wardrobe are displayed in their very own showcase.

In 1979 all 15 Cattley toys were donated to the museum by the last surviving member of the family, Miss Maud Cattley of Ealing, West London. She was 94 years old and felt it was time her beautiful toys found a new home. The museum proved an

Above: Baby, Polly, Pumpie and Tommy on the beach,
painted by N. Cattley (1906)
Below: Tommy, Roompie, Pumpie, Jack, Tittie and Baby Georgie,
painted by C. Cattley (1908)

Like the other Cattley toys he wears an original outfit made in the early 1900s.

Pumpie is shown sitting between the open pages of the Cattley watercolour album at a picture painted by Edith Louise Cattley in 1906, when the elephant was in his prime and had a fine pair of large felt ears. Sadly all that remains of the missing ears today is a small line of stitches across Pumpie's head. The smart naval uniform which Pumpie wears was hand-sewn from dark blue wool and on the jacket are several uneven rows of brass buttons stitched on by young Nellie. The outfit comes complete with waistcoat, white flannel shirt and a small tie. Pumpie has two other costumes in his wardrobe, a white sailor suit and a Highland dress, so the distinguished elephant can be correctly attired for any occasion.

ideal choice as not a day passes without children and their parents being captivated by this charming collection.

Pumpie the elephant, made circa 1900, is the founding member of the Cattley family toys. Pumpie is believed to have been homemade and belonged to the youngest daughter of the family, Helen Edith, known as Nellie. The elephant was made from dark grey felt and filled with wood-wool.

THE BEAR ESSENTIALS — CATTLEY FAMILY TOYS

DATE OF BIRTH:
Circa 1906 made in Germany

HEIGHT
Average height is 9in or 23 cm

FUR TYPE:
Mohair, except for rabbits
which are made from airbrushed velveteen

DISTINGUISHING FEATURES
All toys are in exceptional condition
and most have several original hand-sewn outfits

— CLARENDON BEARS—

Courtesy of the National Trust of Australia, Clarendon Committee, Tasmania, Australia.

BOTH LITTLE Clarendon bears belonged to Kathleen Cocker who was born in 1901 in Devonport, Tasmania, Australia. Kathleen's grandfather, David Cocker, was an early settler in Tasmania and Kathleen and her sisters, Mollie and Margaret, would often gather around the fireside with the teddy bears and listen as their grandfather told exciting stories of pioneer days in Tasmania.

The Cocker sisters lived in Tasmania all their lives and Kathleen possessed an extensive knowledge of the area. She wrote and illustrated the book *Early Houses of the North West Coast of Tasmania* which featured her charming watercolour paintings accompanied by interesting details and anecdotes about the families who once owned the houses.

Kathleen was also renowned for her beautiful

Top left:
From left to right, The Cocker sisters, Marjorie and Mollie with Kathleen, the bears' owner (early 1900s)
Below left:
The Cocker family home in East Devonport (TAS) Australia, painted by Kathleen Cocker
Right: Here one of the Clarendon Bears examines a wheeled bear also from the Clarendon House Collection

needlework which was exhibited several times in England. A pretty hand-smocked dress, still worn by one of the teddy bears, is a fine example of her work.

The Cocker sisters retained a lifelong interest in the preservation of Devonport and during 1974 Kathleen donated several items to the National Trust of Tasmania including her teddy bears. Both Kathleen's teddies now live in the National Trust property Clarendon House, an impressive Georgian-style house built in 1838.

The little bears sit side-by-side upstairs in the nursery, as close as any sisters could be.

THE BEAR ESSENTIALS – CLARENDON BEARS

DATE OF BIRTH:
1906 made in Germany

HEIGHT:
12 in or 31 cm

FUR TYPE:
Short golden coloured bristle mohair, good condition

FILLING:
Excelsior/wood-wool, filled very firmly

EYES AND EARS:
Original black boot-button eyes; small ears set across side seams of head

HEAD CHARACTERISTICS:
Simple construction, straight arms and legs; all paw pads replaced with brown velvet

DISTINGUISHING FEATURES:
Slightly lopsided appearance to mouth of bear in blue dress; all paw pads on both bears replaced with brown velvet

29

—CLOWN BEAR—

Courtesy of Judy and John Sparrow, The Bear Museum, Petersfield, Hants, England.

JUDY SPARROW'S bear museum situated in Petersfield, England is an Aladdin's Cave of interesting teddy bears and dolls. Judy displays her beautiful collection with style and generosity. All voluntary donations are sent to charity and the visitors' book is always full of rapturous praise. Judy is a well-respected authority on the teddy bear and has written several books on the subject. She also makes artist bears, one of which has the engaging name of Bumbletoes.

Teddy bear experts are agreed on one point, a bear's expression is paramount. Simply by the tilt of a woollen nose or the glint of a cheeky glass eye the price paid for a charismatic old teddy bear may soar at toy auctions and amount to a small fortune. Clown Bear, circa 1910, has this very kind of appeal. Although he sits alongside many other veteran teddy bears his long bear snout and unusual wide stitched nose combine with a winsome expression to make him a particular favourite at The Bear Museum.

Judy purchased Clown Bear in 1985 from London teddy bear dealer and author Pam Hebbs. When Clown Bear arrived at the museum his stomach was badly sagged and Judy painstakingly restored him. This gave her the opportunity to carefully inspect him internally. Judy firmly believes that one often learns more about the origin of a bear from the manufacturing details concealed inside the toy. When the inspection was completed it confirmed Clown Bear was definitely of German origin, although not a famous Steiff bear.

Restored to his former glory the old bear was given a bright red theatrical ruff and nobody but Clown Bear could wear it with such panache!

In 1993 a burglary took place at the Petersfield Bear Museum and unfortunately Clown Bear was amongst the bears stolen. He remains at large in the community, sorely missed by everyone.

THE BEAR ESSENTIALS – THE CLOWN BEAR

DATE OF BIRTH:
Pre 1910
made in Germany

HEIGHT:
21 in or 53 cm

FUR TYPE:
Golden coloured mohair,
good quality, fur matted
on head from wear

FILLING:
Excelsior/wood-wool

EYES AND EARS:
Small, black, boot-button
eyes, set close together;
large ears set into side
seam of head

HEAD CHARACTERISTICS:
Very long muzzle, shaved;
unusual wide stitched nose,
vertically stitched with
elongated stitch on either side

BODY CHARACTERISTICS:
Humped back; very long curved
arms; paw pads covered
with original brushed cotton,
five stitched claws; shaped legs
with very long feet; foot pads
worn exposing original canvas
interlining underneath

**DISTINGUISHING
FEATURES:**
Distinctive wide nose stitching;
small, deep set eyes

—Como Bear—

*Gift of Mrs E. Dacey, Richmond, Victoria, to Como House,
South Yarra, Victoria. Model for drawing by courtesy
of the National Trust, Victoria, Australia.*

Left: Como House,
Melbourne, Australia,
once the Armytage
home

JUST SIX kilometres from the heart of Melbourne,
Victoria, Australia you can visit Como Bear at
Como House, a beautiful National Trust property.

Como House was built during 1847 for Charles
and Helen Armytage who had a family of 10 children
born between the years 1858 and 1875. The beautiful
gardens of the house spread over many acres of land
and provided the Armytage children with a magical setting
in which to play. Unlike most children of their era, the
Armytage children were at liberty to romp in the gardens.

Como House hosted many Armytage family occasions
including christenings, weddings and formal garden parties.

The Bear Essentials – Como Bear

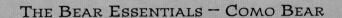

Date of Birth:
1910 probably made
in Germany

Height:
12 in or 30 cm

Fur Type:
Brownish-green short spiky
mohair, fair condition

Filling:
Excelsior/wood-wool filled,
tightly packed

Eyes and Ears:
Eyes are small black boot-
buttons, original; small ears
set into the side seams of
bear's head

**Head
Characteristics:**
Pointed snout, nose stitched
horizontally, original

**Body
Characteristics:**
Good quality toy; small hump
on back; arms curved at
bottom, paw pads replaced
with green velvet, evidence of
five claws on each paw

**Distinguishing
Features:**
Half of bear's
mouth missing

The property remained in the family until 1959 when the two remaining daughters, Constance and Leila, made a generous arrangement with the National Trust to ensure their beloved Como House would be preserved for the nation.

An upstairs bedroom in the house has been styled as a Victorian children's nursery and contains an interesting collection of antique toys. The decorative wallpaper is a reproduction of that used in 1820 for the nursery at Kensington Palace, London which was occupied by Princess (later Queen) Victoria. It provides a delightful backdrop for little Como Bear, who sits high on the mantelpiece in his own wicker chair. Both the bear and his chair were donated by Mrs Edna Dacey who was born in Richmond, Victoria in 1903. As Edna Dacey had no children she kindly bequeathed her bear to the National Trust so he could join the toy collection at Como House.

Como Bear sits upright in his chair, with spiky mohair fur and bright button eyes. He is a cheeky little fellow — how the Armytage children of Como House would have loved him.

–DED TED–

Private Collection. Courtesy of Alison, Grant, Katie and Michael, Melbourne, Victoria, Australia.

DED TED is fortunately very much alive, despite some daring adventures and a close call with the garbage collection.

One hot summer's day in 1986, Alison and her family moved to an old house in Fitzroy, Melbourne, Australia. It had been a long, tiring day and as the family entered the garden of their new home they faced an enormous pile of rubbish. It had been left behind by the previous owners of the house, described by the neighbours as "punks".

The disheartened family stared at the mess and then Alison noticed something leaning against a pile of cardboard boxes. Pushing away some rubbish she pulled out an old and very shabby teddy bear covered in dirt and wearing a small red sweater embroidered with the letters DED TED.

Alison recalls that the bear "tried to look brave" but was probably terrified at the thought of the garbage collection. What a relief

it must have been for Ded Ted as he was dusted down, thoroughly inspected and finally hugged —
a sure sign for a bear that he is going to be loved.

All Ded Ted's paws and pads had been replaced and most of his nose was missing, probably as the result of a dog attack, but he was a tough teddy. His long thin arms were patched all over with brown leather and he held his paws curved high in the air, ready for action.

Ded Ted soon settled down in his new home. Alison's children made him a pair of white karate trousers to keep his old legs warm and he sleeps at the bottom of their beds.

The family recently moved house again and they noticed Ded Ted looked rather miserable when the removal van arrived. However he is now part of the family and will never be abandoned again. Placed carefully in a packing case Ded Ted travelled in style to Preston, Melbourne where he continues to practise his karate.

Ded Ted's rescuer, Alison (circa 1950s)

THE BEAR ESSENTIALS — DED TED

DATE OF BIRTH:
1950 probably made in England

HEIGHT:
16 in or 41 cm

FUR TYPE:
Golden coloured mohair, patchy

FILLING:
Body and head filled with wood-wool, arms and legs filled with multi-coloured kapok

EYES AND EARS:
Large glass eyes, original

HEAD CHARACTERISTICS:
Bear's snout was missing, now repaired with new nose added

BODY CHARACTERISTICS:
Round body; long thin arms; original squeaker mechanism still in operation; paws repaired with leather, originally beige rexine

DISTINGUISHING FEATURES:
Nose repaired; curved arms patched with leather; still wears the red sweater in which he was found, with DED TED stitched across front

35

—THE EDINBURGH BEARS—

Public Collection. Museum of Childhood, Edinburgh, Scotland.

SITUATED ON the historic Royal Mile, in the heart of Edinburgh, is the Museum of Childhood. It was once dubbed "The Noisiest Museum in the World" by a visiting American curator, because many of the old toys are maintained in working order and so click, whir and chime with delightful regularity.

The museum was founded in 1955 by Patrick Murray, a brilliant publicist who had a passion for collecting toys. A softly spoken and genial bachelor, Murray deliberately cultivated a humorous reputation for disliking children and when asked by the press if he liked children Murray smoothly replied "Not between meals". Patrick Murray's generosity and infectious enthusiasm were the main force behind this fascinating museum. The five museum galleries resemble a magical toy department store and are home to a large display of old teddy bears.

The bear seated on the left dates from 1915 and wears

his original knitted turquoise suit with a red and white scarf tied casually around his neck. He has lost much of his stuffing and leans gratefully against his companion, a veteran teddy from the First World War. This old soldier bear, made in 1908, is dressed in the uniform of the Edinburgh Company Royal Army Medical Corps Volunteers. The bear's uniform would have been carefully hand-sewn by his original owner during the First World War. Teddy bears often reflect social history and many bears of this period were equipped with extensive wartime uniforms. The old soldier seems to remember his military training and, although his elderly knees are now a little wobbly, he still stands firmly to attention.

THE BEAR ESSENTIALS — BEAR IN TURQUOISE KNITTED SUIT

DATE OF BIRTH:
1915

HEIGHT:
13 in or 33 cm

FUR TYPE:
Golden coloured
mohair plush, fair condition

FILLING:
Excelsior/wood-wool

EYES AND EARS:
Original wooden boot-button
type eyes, black; ears set
below head seam

HEAD
CHARACTERISTICS:
Prominent snout,
black silk embroidered nose;
mouth stitching missing

BODY
CHARACTERISTICS:
Small hump on back; long arms,
paw pads replaced

DISTINGUISHING FEATURES:
The bear's long arms have twisted
slightly due to misplaced stuffing,
the result being his paws now
turn outwards; wears original
knitted suit and scarf

THE BEAR ESSENTIALS — SOLDIER BEAR

DATE OF BIRTH:
1908

HEIGHT:
13 in or 33 cm

FUR TYPE:
Light golden coloured
mohair plush, very worn

FILLING:
Excelsior/wood-wool

EYES AND EARS:
Black wooden button eyes,
original; ears set well apart
and centrally across head seam

HEAD
CHARACTERISTICS:
Prominent pointed snout,
light tan silk nose, very worn;
mouth stitching missing

BODY
CHARACTERISTICS:
Typical early bear, hump on his back
and long limbs; all paw pads
replaced, foot pads with tan sateen

DISTINGUISHING FEATURES:
A well loved bear, his uniform
covers the patches on his body;
strange upturned feet, due to wear

This cheerful bear also hails from the Museum of Childhood. He is wearing white pyjamas

—ELSIE'S BEAR—

Private Collection. Courtesy of the Owner, Victoria, Australia.

ELSIE'S BEAR sits proudly wearing his prize winning rosette, awarded for winning The Oldest and Most Interesting Teddy Bear competition held in 1991 at Rippon Lea, a National Trust property in Victoria, Australia.

The little bear was made in 1910 and belonged to Elsie Lilian MacLean who was born in Bermondsey, London in 1911. Elsie was the only child of Peter and Louisa MacLean and she enjoyed a carefree childhood until 1914 when the First World War broke out and her father enlisted to serve with the 6th Battalion Lincolnshire Regiment. Sadly, on 4th October 1917, the family received the tragic news that Peter MacLean had been killed by a landmine while on active service. He was buried in Passchendaele, Belgium. Elsie was just six years old at the time and her teddy bear, the last gift from her beloved father, would be a poignant reminder of him all her life.

After the death of Peter MacLean his family suffered considerable financial hardship. Eventually Elsie's mother managed to find employment which, combined with her meagre widow's pension, enabled her to rent two small rooms in London. Elsie recalls that instead of wardrobes their clothes were stored in wooden fruit boxes and that the clothes wringer held pride of place at the end of their bed. New clothes and toys were a rarity and the small pair of leather shoes in the picture on the previous page were Elsie's "best ones" as a child and she kept them long after they had been outgrown.

Elsie's bear, like many early teddy bears, had a prominent hump on his back and Elsie recalls that as a child she was curious about this feature. Thinking it was a deformity of some kind she would try to pinch it off ! The much-loved bear's brown felt paws eventually wore out so Elsie's mother

Right:
Elsie MacLean
(back, centre)
and her cousins
— the youngest
holds Elsie's bear

Far Right:
Elsie MacLean
with her parents
(1916)

repaired them with some scraps of fabric from her work basket, however, Elsie recalls being unappreciative as she was not at all sure a bear should have *blue* paws.

Elsie grew up and married in 1936. She had two daughters and the whole family emigrated to Australia where the bear now lives with Elsie's daughter, Hilary. Since his outstanding success in the teddy competition Elsie's Bear has become quite a celebrity and now considers it discourteous of anyone to even think a bear's paws should be anything *but* blue.

THE BEAR ESSENTIALS — ELSIE'S BEAR

DATE OF BIRTH:
1910 made in Germany

HEIGHT:
12 in or 31 cm

FUR TYPE:
Dark brown mohair

FILLING:
Excelsior/wood-wool

EYES AND EARS:
Black boot-button type, original

HEAD CHARACTERISTICS:
Upturned muzzle, shaved; ears set below seam on head; nose and mouth stitching badly worn.

BODY CHARACTERISTICS:
Humped back; long arms with curved paws; right paw pad and feet pads repaired with blue cotton fabric, left paw pad in black cotton (original pads felt), few remains of claw stitching

DISTINGUISHING FEATURES:
Distinctive blue paws

—Fire Guard Bear—

Courtesy of the Cotswold Teddy Bear Museum, Broadway, Cotswolds, England (Museum closed March 1995).

Early postcard of child
in a toy fire-engine

THIS RARE 1906 Steiff teddy was once
the mascot of the London Fire Brigade.
The plucky bear experienced several
years of active fire-fighting service
during the London Blitz in the
Second World War.

Each night as fierce bombing
raids sparked fires all over
London, Fire Guard Bear, as

an enthusiastic member of the brigade, would accompany his crew in their fire engine as it sped around the darkened streets to fight the fires. No blaze was too large or fierce for Fire Guard Bear to tackle. Only once did his enthusiasm wane, just a little — when he got too close to the action and his feet began to singe. Fortunately the smell of burning wool was noticed by his crew who quickly extinguished poor Fire Guard's smoking paws. The London Fire Brigade was so impressed with Fire Guard's courage it awarded him two Bomb Reconnaissance armbands and a large "FIRE GUARD" bib to wear.

After the war Fire Guard Bear retired from active service and now lives at the Cotswold Teddy Bear Museum with many other teddy bears, including Fritz the war veteran and Horatio the Haunted, featured on pages 44 and 60 respectively.

Always on the alert for a trail of smoke Fire Guard Bear remembers his fire drill and would quickly spring into action should the need arise.

THE BEAR ESSENTIALS — FIRE GUARD BEAR

DATE OF BIRTH:
1906 Steiff bear made in Germany

HEIGHT:
23 in or 58 cm

FUR TYPE:
Light golden coloured mohair in good condition

FILLING:
Excelsior/wood-wool

EYES AND EARS:
Black boot-button eyes; rounded ears set wide apart

HEAD CHARACTERISTICS:
Rare centre seam on head; nose restitched with black silk

BODY CHARACTERISTICS:
Original felt paws and pads, some repaired; long arms and large feet

DISTINGUISHING FEATURES:
Paw pads have burnt and singed areas, due to his active service; he wears fire service armbands and bib; he also has a rare centre seam on his head – a device employed by Steiff to save valuable fabric

—FORBY—

*Private Collection. Courtesy of the Owner,
Melbourne, Victoria, Australia.*

FORBY, the most favoured of bears, cannot help but be noticed in a crowd for he stands an impressive 32 in or 81 cm tall and has the kind of expression which attracts bear lovers of every age, all of whom long to take him home.

Huge Forby was made circa 1909 and, although he is believed to be of English origin, he was discovered in the old gold mining district of Ballarat in Victoria, Australia. He was found slumped in a dusty corner looking the picture of sartorial elegance wearing a blue velvet dinner jacket complete with bow tie and, surprisingly, an old daisy chain hanging over one ear.

Forby had obviously been a much loved toy as he was patched all over and his fur was worn from continuous cuddles.

Little is known of Forby's history except that a bear of his size and quality would no doubt have been an expensive toy in 1909. Perhaps he was purchased as the result of some good luck on the Victorian goldfields, where fortunes were often made overnight by a successful find.

A Forby admirer recently presented the bear with a Retired Service League badge which Forby now has proudly pinned to his blue jacket. Ever modest, Forby takes public acclaim in his stride and never, ever appears to suffer from conceit.

Above: Early postcard of Ballarat, Australia, where Forby was found

Left: Children playing on a farm at Ballarat

THE BEAR ESSENTIALS — FORBY

DATE OF BIRTH:
1909 probably made in England

HEIGHT:
32 in or 81 cm

FUR TYPE:
Light blonde mohair, worn condition

FILLING:
Excelsior/wood-wool

EYES AND EARS:
Black button eyes, not original; ears possibly moved from their original position

HEAD CHARACTERISTICS:
Large wide head, long shaved snout; restitched nose

BODY CHARACTERISTICS:
Prominent hump on back; very long arms; distinct curve at paws; all paw pads repaired with beige cotton; unusual bell-shaped feet, soles lined with thick board; old lead weight tilt growler box.

DISTINGUISHING FEATURES:
Distinctive shape to feet; large size

43

—FRITZ—

Public Collection. Courtesy of the Cotswold Teddy Bear Museum, Broadway, Cotswolds, England (Museum closed March 1995).

FRITZ IS only a small bear but his diminutive size is more than made up for by his bravery.

Little Fritz was discovered at the end of the Second World War. He was tucked beneath the floorboards of a Nissen hut in England where he had been hidden by his owner, a German prisoner of war. At the end of the war the German soldier was repatriated and, amid all the confusion, he forgot his little bear which was later found by British troops. When Fritz was pulled from beneath the floor he was a little worn and dusty but was still wearing his knitted jacket, to which was pinned an impressive collection of military badges.

Standing nearby holding the stars and stripes is Buddy, another bear with a wartime origin. Buddy was made in 1930 and brought to England by his owner, an American serviceman who was stationed at Burtonwood US Airbase

near Warrington. The serviceman fell in love with a local girl named Penny Ashton. They became engaged and, before he left to take part in the D-Day landings, he gave Buddy to his betrothed. Tragically the serviceman was killed and Buddy never left Penny's side until her death in 1983.

In wartime few other toys have provided the solace of a teddy bear. Despite grim circumstances teddy bears were a comforting reminder of home for young and old, from the youngest child evacuees who waved goodbye to their parents while clutching a teddy bear, to the many brave servicemen who regarded their bears as the ultimate talisman.

The bears until recently, lived peacefully at the Cotswold Teddy Bear Museum, in the pretty village of Broadway. The poignant wartime stories of Buddy and Fritz serve to remind us of the enormous sacrifice many brave soldiers made throughout the war: *Lest we forget.*

THE BEAR ESSENTIALS – FRITZ

DATE OF BIRTH:
1906 Steiff bear made in Germany

HEIGHT:
11 in or 28 cm

FUR TYPE:
Light golden coloured mohair, worn and discoloured

FILLING:
Excelsior/wood-wool

EYES AND EARS:
Round, brown boot-button eyes; rounded ears set over head seams

HEAD CHARACTERISTICS:
Head, misshapen with wear; black vertical stitched nose, worn

BODY CHARACTERISTICS:
Original pads and claws still visible

DISTINGUISHING FEATURES:
Fritz's wonderful collection of German and British badges and military insignia pinned onto a knitted grey and pink jacket

THE BEAR ESSENTIALS – BUDDY

DATE OF BIRTH:
Circa 1930 made in the United States by the Ideal Toy Company

HEIGHT:
18 in or 46 cm

FUR TYPE:
Bright golden coloured mohair

FILLING:
Excelsior

EYES
Still has original glass eyes

HEAD CHARACTERISTICS:
Large cupped ears, set across head seams of bear

BODY CHARACTERISTICS:
Long limbs with upturned paws and large feet, original paw pads, claws missing

DISTINGUISHING FEATURES:
Buddy has distinctive spoon-shaped paws

—Gertrude's Bear—

Private collection. Courtesy of the Owner, Melbourne, Victoria, Australia.

THE SMALL bear sitting on the teacup belonged to Gertrude Fanny Herbertson, who was born in 1884 in Melbourne, Victoria, Australia. Gertrude was the eldest child of five children who were orphaned when both parents fell victim to tuberculosis. Her aunt and uncle, Sarah and Joseph Porter, adopted Gertrude and in 1902 she travelled to their home in Portland, Victoria.

Portland was a busy seafaring town during the early 1900s and Joseph and Sarah owned a thriving business named The General Household Furniture and Mattrass Warehouse (sic), which, as the name implies, sold quite a wide range of goods. The couple enjoyed their niece's company as Gertrude was a bright, happy girl who helped her aunt and uncle run their business. Gertrude was also accomplished at needlework and lacemaking and examples of her beautiful work became treasured family heirlooms, along with her little teddy bear who was purchased from the Porters' store.

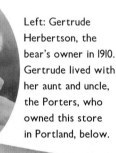

Left: Gertrude Herbertson, the bear's owner in 1910. Gertrude lived with her aunt and uncle, the Porters, who owned this store in Portland, below.

Gertrude's Bear, circa 1906, is a fine example of early teddy bear manufacture. Constructed in a primitive manner the bear's arms and legs were jointed with wire rods finished with external discs. He has a distinctive pointed snout and, despite the loss of an ear, he is a most appealing little character.

When Gertrude died the bear was left to her son Alan and his wife Kathleen. Gertrude's Bear now sits in the china cabinet in Alan and Kathleen's lounge room and, being such a convenient size, the teddy bear occasionally enjoys an outing tucked in Alan's top pocket. As Alan and Kathleen have five children and 10 grandchildren the little bear's happy future seems well and truly guaranteed.

THE BEAR ESSENTIALS – GERTRUDE'S BEAR

DATE OF BIRTH:
1906

HEIGHT:
6 in or 15 cm

FUR TYPE:
Short bristle type golden coloured mohair, patchy

FILLING:
Excelsior/wood-wool, firmly packed

EYES AND EARS:
Original, small, round, black glass eyes; ears very small, sewn on to surface of head, right ear missing

HEAD CHARACTERISTICS:
Unusual construction, short side seams run up from neck joint to just under ears, a third seam runs up centrally from neck joint to under the bear's long muzzle; eyes placed close together; nose stitching worn

BODY CHARACTERISTICS:
Simple body construction with side seams only, gathered slightly on shoulder line and between legs; legs and arms articulate with wire rods finished with external discs; straight legs; slight curve to arms, no paw pads, no claw stitching

DISTINGUISHING FEATURES:
Minus right ear

—GILLIAN'S BEAR—

Private Collection. Courtesy of the Owner, Melbourne, Victoria, Australia.

GILLIAN WAS given her teddy bear in 1934 on her second birthday. When she was five years old her parents separated and it was decided that Gillian should attend boarding school. Gillian's teddy bear accompanied her to school and, at a time when adult behaviour seemed inexplicable to the little girl, the bear became her greatest comfort. Teddy and Gillian faced the day-to-day rigours of English boarding school together and eventually adjusted to their new life away from home.

Teddy remained a great favourite for many years, only having to share Gillian's affections when Margie, a large china doll, arrived in 1941.

It seems a certain rivalry existed between the two toys and eventually, like many bears before him, teddy was packed away in a trunk where he spent many sad years completely forgotten.

In 1960 Gillian emigrated to Australia with her husband and three young children. The old trunk crossed the seas with the family but was not opened until

Gillian, the bear's owner, as a baby (circa 1933)

many years later. When the trunk was finally reopened Margie the doll was discovered and poor old teddy was found at the very bottom of the trunk, cold, squashed and in two pieces as his head had fallen off!

Gillian was most concerned to see her old friend in such a bad way. She carefully wrapped up the squashed pieces of her bear and took them to a teddy bear hospital where teddy's head was mended, his body restuffed and a new growler installed. Many years before, Gillian's brother had pulled out the bear's eyes so, whilst in hospital, teddy also received a new set of amber glass eyes.

Gillian is now a grandmother and in her spare time makes beautiful patchwork quilts and baby clothes which teddy occasionally models for her. However much of the bear's time is spent watching television from a comfy chair in the lounge room which he shares with his old friend and rival, Margie the china doll.

THE BEAR ESSENTIALS — GILLIAN'S BEAR

DATE OF BIRTH:
1934 made in England

HEIGHT:
20 in or 51 cm

FUR TYPE:
Golden coloured mohair

FILLING:
Excelsior/wood-wool

EYES AND EARS:
Amber glass eyes, not original; ears well spaced

HEAD CHARACTERISTICS:
Round head, characteristic of English teddy bears; vertical stitched nose, original

BODY CHARACTERISTICS:
Round body; fairly short arms, cotton twill paw pads, three claws

DISTINGUISHING FEATURES:
Designer patchwork clothes and matching sweater

—THE GOOD-TIME TED AND FRIENDS—

Courtesy of Arundel Toy and Military Museum, Arundel, West Sussex, England.

SITUATED IN West Sussex, England and just a hop and a skip from historic Arundel Castle, which dates back to pre-Roman times, is the Arundel Toy and Military Museum where twin bears Theo and Edward, Durban Ted, Knobby and the wonderful Good-time Ted live.

Dancing together on the facing page are the twins, Theo and Edward, who once belonged to Ingrid Legat, an author of children's stories. Theo and Edward began life as identical teddy bears but have aged quite differently over the years. Ingrid recalls that as a child she would partner Theo for wild dances, swinging the bear around her head in time to the music which would explain his rather long arms. Both bears have been patched all over and still wear their original practical blue corduroy overalls.

Durban Ted, pictured on page 53, travelled to England from South Africa with his owner some 45 years ago. He arrived wearing his original outfit — a grey fur coat, black rubber boots and a thick woollen scarf which was considered rather excessive, considering the warm climate in South Africa.

Knobby Bear is a mystery. Pictured on page 52 with the Good-time Ted, he simply arrived at the museum one day wearing a silver bell around his neck. His claim to fame is his extraordinary knobby knees. As for the large bear dressed in blue and nicknamed the Good-time Ted, he wears his beret on a jaunty angle and no-one dares guess his pedigree as it seems he has always been much too busy having a GOOD TIME!

Early postcard of Arundel Castle, West Sussex, England

THE BEAR ESSENTIALS –

THEO AND EDWARD

HEIGHT:
Both 15 in or 38 cm

DISTINGUISHING FEATURES:
Very patched twin bears, Theo wears cloth helmet stitched on to his head and has much longer arms than Edward, both wear original blue corduroy overalls, Edward has a red knitted top.

DURBAN TED

HEIGHT:
12 in or 31 cm

DISTINGUISHING FEATURES:
Extensive winter wardrobe

KNOBBY

HEIGHT:
14 in or 36 cm

DISTINGUISHING FEATURES:
Strange bent knees, dressed in original red knitted sweater with silver bell tied around his neck

GOOD-TIME TED

HEIGHT:
20 in or 51 cm

DISTINGUISHING FEATURES:
Large early bear, long limbs, dressed in a blue party suit tied with red ribbon and matching beret

~GROWL~

Private collection. Courtesy of the Owner, Melbourne, Victoria, Australia.

Above: Postcard of Collins St,
Melbourne, Australia, the street
where Growl was purchased
Right: Frank, Growl's owner,
aged six (1914)

HANDSOME GROWL bear belonged to Frank and was given his name because as a young bear, when placed in a seated position, he would usually topple over and give a thundering growl of protest.

Frank's father, a businessman from Perth, Western Australia, purchased Growl in 1907 whilst on a business trip to Melbourne, Victoria, Australia. Hoping to find a gift to take home for his wife, who was expecting their first child, he visited Hicks Atkinson, a large department store that was situated in the exclusive Collins Street area of the city.

At the time, teddy bears were the latest novelty, so when Frank's father saw handsome Growl sitting on a shelf he decided the teddy bear would make an ideal gift for his new child. The purchase proved unusually difficult as the bear was the very last one in the store and staff were reluctant to sell him before their new shipment of teddy bears arrived. However, the manager of the store was eventually persuaded and Growl was packed securely and taken home to Perth to await the birth of his new owner.

Frank was born in April 1908 and, to his parents' amusement, the teddy bear was considerably larger than their new baby son. Growl soon became Frank's favourite toy, together

54

with a large Steiff elephant and a dog on wheels.

Growl and Frank have been together all their lives except for a period during the Second World War when Frank served in the R.A.F.

Frank and his wife Peggy are now retired and have lived in the same beautiful house in a leafy suburb of Melbourne for more than 60 years. Frank has kept his childhood companions and is very pleased the toys have stood the test of time so well, especially Growl who still manages a faint grumble when tipped over.

THE BEAR ESSENTIALS – GROWL BEAR

DATE OF BIRTH:
1907 made in England

HEIGHT:
24 in or 61 cm

FUR TYPE:
Long, wavy, golden coloured mohair, good quality

FILLING:
Excelsior/wood-wool, filled firmly

EYES AND EARS:
Original glass eyes; black vertical stitched nose, extended stitch at each side of nose; mouth stitching missing.

HEAD CHARACTERISTICS:
Large broad head; prominent snout, shaved

BODY CHARACTERISTICS:
Solid body; growl still works faintly; humped back; long arms, well shaped legs; both paws and left foot pad replaced with woollen cloth, right foot repaired with chamois leather

DISTINGUISHING FEATURES:
Slightly lopsided appearance to Growl's head; left ear appears to be placed lower than right ear

—HATBOX BEAR—

*Private Collection. Courtesy of the Harvey family,
Australia and England.*

THE HATBOX Bear was one of a group of
bears which belonged to the Harvey
family who lived in London in the 1940s.
Hatbox, who always wore a pair of baggy
blue trousers, was originally known to the
children simply as Teddy Blue Trousers.

Purchased from a London street market
circa 1945 the teddy bear was considered a
fortunate find because, due to the Second
World War, toys were not freely available in
London. Hatbox was given to the eldest
Harvey child but eventually, as wartime
shortages eased, each of the Harvey children received a
teddy of their own and soon Hatbox had plenty
of company.

Despite a hectic social life Hatbox Bear has always
looked very miserable. The children recall that they felt
sorry for his sad face and gave him starring roles in all

their games hoping to cheer him up. However the bear's woollen mouth remained firmly downturned, his loose glass eye drooped further and it seemed no amount of treats could make Hatbox smile.

The bear emigrated to Australia with some of the Harvey family in the 1960s and he now lives in a very smart hatbox, hence his new name. He still wears his original 1940s blue trousers and, although his expression could hardly be described as joyful, the family believe that the sunshine has had a beneficial effect on his disposition.

THE BEAR ESSENTIALS — HATBOX BEAR

DATE OF BIRTH:
1945 made in England, possibly by Ealon toys

HEIGHT:
15 in or 38 cm

FUR TYPE:
Pale golden coloured mohair

FILLING:
Kapok

EYES AND EARS:
Large glass eyes; ears inserted into the head across side seam

HEAD CHARACTERISTICS:
Rather flat face; small original nose with horizontal stitch

BODY CHARACTERISTICS:
Limbs not articulated; unusual construction with two seams down centre of body; squeaker in body no longer working; original twill paws, no claws

DISTINGUISHING FEATURES:
Rather unhappy expression; small black woollen dot below mouth

—HILDA'S BEAR—

Courtesy of The Lilliput Antique Doll and Toy Museum, Brading, Isle of Wight, England.

THIS BEAR, made in 1906, lives at The Lilliput Doll Museum on the beautiful Isle of Wight. The little bear is a great favourite of the museum's founder as he once belonged to her mother, Hilda Western.

Hilda May Western was born in England in 1900 and her cousins, Ken and George Western, were famous comedians of the day. Known as "The Western Brothers" the pair made the little girl laugh and she confided in them her desire for a teddy bear. Hilda carefully saved up her pocket money and, with a little help from her cousins, bought her teddy bear from a travelling English fair for a few pence.

Hilda treasured her teddy bear and after she married and had a young family of her own she considered him much too precious to be played with. Despite the pleas of her children to hold him, the bear was placed high on a shelf, beyond the reach of small hands.

Eventually teddy was inherited by Hilda's daughter, Margaret, and the fortunate bear came out of retirement to enjoy a new and busy lease on life at the Lilliput Toy Museum. Margaret is the founder of the museum and she frequently gives talks on the subject of antique toys. When visiting schools she always takes along her mother's bear to demonstrate the differences between old and modern day teddy bears. Recalling her own childhood desire to touch the little bear she generously allows the children to examine him, first inquiring "Who is very gentle?".

There is always an enthusiastic flurry of small hands and Hilda's bear is passed

THE BEAR ESSENTIALS — HILDA'S BEAR

DATE OF BIRTH:
1905 probably made in Germany

HEIGHT:
11 in or 33 cm

FUR TYPE:
Golden coloured mohair, very worn

FILLING:
Kapok in head, excelsior/
wood-wool in body

EYES AND EARS:
Small black boot-button eyes,
original; ears sewn below the side
seam on head

HEAD CHARACTERISTICS:
Long, pointed muzzle; remains of
horizontally stitched nose; mouth
stitching worn

BODY CHARACTERISTICS:
Pronounced hump on back; long
curved paws; limbs attached
with external boot-buttons; long
feet; original felt paw pads;
growler not operative

**DISTINGUISHING
FEATURES:**
Hole on left side of bear's face
exposing kapok filling; limbs
attached by buttons

carefully around the classroom to the delight of the children, who gently stroke his old fur and note the characteristics of an old bear — long thin arms, humped back and bright boot-button eyes.

Margaret enjoys watching the faces of the children who appreciate the opportunity to touch this precious old toy and also learn the value of conservation. Hilda's Bear seems to enjoy himself as well and the old veteran never fails to leave a school without a glint in his eye.

–Horatio the Haunted–

Public Collection. Courtesy of the Cotswold Teddy Bear Museum, Broadway, Cotswolds, England (Museum closed March 1995).

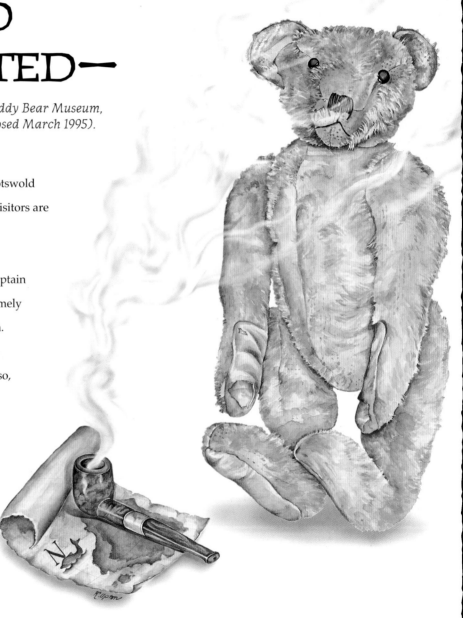

HORATIO THE Haunted is a celebrity at the Cotswold Teddy Bear Museum and parties of museum visitors are often found engrossed in reading his intriguing and supernatural history.

Horatio dates from 1910 and belonged to a sea captain named Thomas Milligan. Captain Milligan was extremely fond of Horatio and regarded the bear as his talisman. Like many sailors the Captain was very superstitious and as a result he refused to set sail without his bear so, for many years, Horatio accompanied Captain Milligan on his travels.

Horatio's mysterious reputation began in 1951, after Captain Milligan's death, when Horatio had been adopted by Milligan's nephew, Frederick Chalkley. Chalkley began to notice strange and supernatural happenings occurring in the proximity of Horatio and in a letter to an auctioneer he wrote:

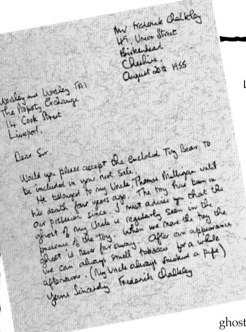

Mr Frederick Chalkley
49 Union Street
Birkenhead
Cheshire
August 20th 1955

Worsley and Worsley FAI
The Property Exchange
14 Cook Street
Liverpool.

Dear Sir,

Would you please accept the Enclosed Toy Bear to be included in your next Sale. He belonged to my Uncle Thomas Milligan until his death four years ago. The toy has been in our possession since. I must advise you that the ghost of my Uncle is regularly seen in the presence of the Toy. When we move the toy the ghost is never far away. After an appearance we can always smell tobacco for a while afterwards. (My Uncle always smoked a pipe.)
Yours Sincerely Frederick Chalkley

Left: Letter from the Captain's nephew to an auctioneer (1955)

"I must advise you that the ghost of my Uncle is regularly seen in the presence of the toy. When we move the toy the ghost is never far away. After an appearance we can always smell tobacco for a while afterwards. (My Uncle always smoked a pipe.)".

Horatio had several owners who all confirmed there was certainly an unusual and inexplicable presence about the bear. Many commented on the aroma which would occasionally surround Horatio, described as sweet and compared to tobacco. However, despite several strange events associated with Horatio, it must

be said that all his owners agreed that the experiences were of a friendly nature and not in the least bit frightening.

In 1991 Horatio was auctioned and shortly afterwards he arrived at the Cotswold Teddy Bear Museum. Horatio settled down happily in his new home, although his new owners have noticed that sometimes, when the doors of the Museum are unlocked of a morning, they smell a hint of tobacco in the air and on other occasions they have heard strange scuffling noises which sound similar to footsteps.

Some friendships are special and it seems the bond forged between Captain Milligan and his bear cannot be broken. Long may Captain Milligan and Horatio sail the seas of time together.

THE BEAR ESSENTIALS – HORATIO BEAR

DATE OF BIRTH:
1910 made in Germany

HEIGHT:
20 in or 51 cm

FUR TYPE:
Golden coloured mohair

FILLING:
Excelsior/wood-wool

EYES AND EARS:
Black boot-button eyes; rounded ears set wide apart

HEAD CHARACTERISTICS:
Broad head; tan vertical stitched nose

BODY CHARACTERISTICS:
Felt paws and pads, some repaired; very long arms and large feet

DISTINGUISHING FEATURES:
The bear has a collection of original letters regarding his history; Horatio has a 'scar' close to the centre seam of his body and is occasionally surrounded by the smell of tobacco!

HMS. HORATIO

─J.T. OR KIM'S BEAR─

*Private Collection. Courtesy of both of the bear's owners,
Gae in South Australia, Australia
and the Lee family in Victoria, Australia.*

MOST TEDDY bears would consider it good fortune to find one happy home in a lifetime, however this lucky bear found two.

Gae was born in Adelaide, South Australia in 1940 and one of her earliest memories is of a passion for teddy bears. As soon as she had learnt to write Gae appealed to Father Christmas for a golden teddy bear. Sadly, due to wartime shortages, her request was even beyond the control of Father Christmas and although pink or blue bears were available Gae had her heart set firmly on a real teddy bear, by which she meant a bear with golden coloured fur.

When she was seven Gae's wish came true. A suitable teddy bear was found in an Adelaide department store called John Martins and the little bear was everything Gae had dreamed of. Made in England by the Merrythought toy company he had a growler, brown glass eyes and, best of all, lots of fluffy, golden fur. Gae still recalls the delight at his arrival and when the happy child was asked what she intended to call her new friend she replied, "Just Teddy", so that was how he was always known. Just Teddy, sometimes abbreviated to J.T., was never far from Gae's side throughout her childhood years. He attended school, slept on her bed and always received a goodnight kiss.

Many years later, when she had grown up, Gae heard that close family friends were also experiencing difficulty in obtaining a teddy bear for their first child. The situation was similar to the one Gae had been in as the new parents were looking for a bear with golden fur. Gae decided to give her beloved bear to the new parents, knowing that he would be well loved. So J.T. came out of retirement and travelled interstate to Victoria, where he became known as Kim's Teddy.

Nowadays the bear and his new family, who are enthusiastic campers, travel many miles to enjoy the beautiful Australian scenery and wildlife and since his adoption the bear has become a most knowledgeable egg watcher.

Left: The bear's first owner, Gae (circa 1943)

Below: The bear's second owner, Kim (1976)

THE BEAR ESSENTIALS — J.T. OR KIM'S BEAR

DATE OF BIRTH:
1947 made in England by the Merrythought Toy Company

HEIGHT:
15 in or 39 cm

FUR TYPE:
Long golden coloured mohair, good condition

FILLING:
Kapok, nose filled with excelsior/wood-wool

EYES AND EARS:
Original glass eyes, right eye stained beneath with glue; ears set across head seams

HEAD CHARACTERISTICS:
Black silk nose, vertically stitched

BODY CHARACTERISTICS:
Straight legs; tan twill paws, original, three claws on each paw; squeaker in body now inoperative

DISTINGUISHING FEATURES:
Glue smudge under right eye; scrap of the original Merrythought label on left foot

—Jan's Teddy—

Private Collection. Courtesy of Jan and family, Glen Waverley, Victoria, Australia.

THIS BEAR, always known simply as Teddy, wears a very sweet expression which could be due to the spirit of goodwill in which he arrived shortly before Jan's birth.

In the hot summer of January 1952 a severe bushfire swept through Greta in rural Victoria, Australia. It caused considerable damage to the countryside as well as surrounding farming properties. Jan's father, Harold Cook, generously assisted a nearby farmer in rebuilding his damaged fences and refused to accept payment for his work. As a token of gratitude the farmer presented the teddy bear to Harold and Helene Cook who were awaiting the birth of their first child.

Later in 1952 their daughter, Jan, was born. The family moved to Milawa, a small Victorian country town and, as toys were not widely available at the time, Jan's bear became a star attraction in the small community. Country children are renowned for their generosity and Jan was no

Jan with her brother and her teddy (circa 1956)

exception. Teddy was her great favourite but she would occasionally allow close friends to borrow him for "an overnight stay at their place". Jan also recalls, with humour, one Christmas when teachers were rehearsing the school's Nativity play. Unable to locate a suitable sized doll to play baby Jesus, Jan's bear auditioned for the part and won the starring role. Teddy appeared tightly swaddled in a blanket to disguise his fur and laid in the manger for all to adore.

The beautiful cream woollen dress that Teddy still wears was knitted in 1952 by Helene Cook for her baby daughter. Teddy's demure appearance could be misleading but Jan is emphatic that "Teddy has always been a boy".

Jan is now married with a family of her own and her bear, after his busy country life, is enjoying a peaceful retirement on a shelf in their living room.

THE BEAR ESSENTIALS – JAN'S TEDDY

DATE OF BIRTH:
1952

HEIGHT:
23 in or 58 cm

FUR TYPE:
Light wavy golden coloured mohair very worn on head

FILLING:
Excelsior/wood-wool for body and head but bottom of paws filled with kapok

EYES AND EARS:
Original large glass eyes, now worn clear but specks of brown paint can still be seen below; large ears set below side seam of head

HEAD CHARACTERISTICS:
Wide head, ears set well apart; stuffing in bear's nose displaced and so gives a dimpled appearance; vertical stitched nose, worked in a triangle shape; no mouth stitching remains

BODY CHARACTERISTICS:
Head and body one piece (not articulated); short curved arms; small rounded feet; original rexine pads, worn condition

DISTINGUISHING FEATURES:
Dimpled nose

—JESSICA BEAR—

Private Collection. Courtesy of the Cockrill Family, England and Australia.

IF A BEAR could have a favourite book then Jessica would certainly choose *The Little Book of Bear Care* as it covers everything that a bear with Jessica's medical history could wish to know.

Jessica Bear belonged to Joan Betts who was born in Norwich, England in 1924. Joan's father was a stationmaster and the family moved frequently to various parts of East Anglia throughout her childhood. Unlike many bears who become male in their owners' imaginations Jessica was always a girl and owned a colourful assortment of dresses and skirts which Joan made for her.

When Joan grew up she married and had three children of her own, Lesley, John and Pauline. Jessica Bear continued to be a family favourite and was played with by each of the children. Doctors and nurses was the children's favourite game and Jessica was usually cast as the patient. On one occasion Pauline, the youngest child, had a serious fall which required several stitches in her forehead. Her brother, John, was obviously inspired by the incident and later performed a 'Growlerectomy' on the long suffering Jessica, stitching several blue sutures down her middle.

Jessica underwent many operations throughout the 1950s, including such major surgery as a right arm replacement.

Perhaps it is no surprise that Pauline Cockrill later grew up to become senior curator of soft toys at the Bethnal Green Museum of Childhood in London, where she specialised in teddy bear history and wrote several books about the teddy bear story.

THE BEAR ESSENTIALS – JESSICA BEAR

DATE OF BIRTH:
1924

HEIGHT:
12 in or 30 cm

FUR TYPE:
Golden coloured mohair, short bristle type,
very worn condition

FILLING:
Excelsior/wood-wool

EYES AND EARS:
Eyes brown woollen stitches, originally
glass; small ears set into head seams
indicative of cheaper made bears

HEAD CHARACTERISTICS:
Nose and mouth stitching missing

BODY CHARACTERISTICS:
Originally externally jointed with metal rods through the top
and lower part of body, ends protruding into the shoulders
and thighs of bear, these have disintegrated and the limbs
have been simply sewn onto body

DISTINGUISHING FEATURES:
Jessica has too many distinguishing features to mention all of
them, however, she once had a squeaker and the dark oval
mark on her chest is the result of it being pushed excessively

As for Jessica, she became a storehouse of precious childhood memories for the Cockrill family who would not dream of changing one patch on her body. Jessica's health improved dramatically once the Cockrill children had grown up and nowadays she has little more to worry about than deciding whether to wear the braces of her skirt inside or outside her sweater.

JOCIE'S LITTLE TED

*Courtesy of The Adams family,
Jocie, Fiona and Sarah,
Melbourne, Victoria, Australia.*

LITTLE TED, a nine-to-five working bear, can often be seen with his nose pressed up against a window of the municipal offices after another busy day assisting his owner with family day care services.

Little Ted and his brother, Big Ted, were both purchased in 1950 from a small toy and drapery store in Carlton, Victoria, Australia. Little Ted arrived in time for Jocie's 10th birthday and Big Ted joined him a little while later when Jocie had broken her wrist and needed cheering up. Both teddies were great favourites in the early days but, like many bears, they spent several years in a dark cupboard until Jocie married and had two daughters of her own, Fiona and Sarah.

Both Jocie's girls loved the teddies but Sarah in particular played with them constantly. It was a common occurrence for Sarah to line up all her teddies in the hallway during the middle of the night for an impromptu tea party, often waking the entire household as she chatted to them over 'tea'. Sarah usually carried Little Ted by his ear which eventually wore loose and fell off and, as the bear gradually became entirely real in Sarah's imagination, Little Ted would patiently take the blame for any and all of her misdeeds.

When Sarah and Fiona had grown up the teddies went to work with Jocie, their original owner. She organised an after school programme where both teddies assisted with story telling and comforting sad children. Unfortunately disaster struck one day when Big Ted disappeared, without trace, from the kindergarten. Believed to have been kidnapped, Big Ted has not been seen again. However Little Ted continues his work stoically. A well respected working bear, he is occasionally seen taking a well-earned cuppa in his tea break.

THE BEAR ESSENTIALS — LITTLE TED

DATE OF BIRTH:
1950 made in Australia,
possibly by Lindee

HEIGHT:
18 in or 46 cm

FUR TYPE:
Gold coloured cotton plush

FILLING:
Excelsior/wood-wool

EYES AND EARS:
Black button eyes;
circular ears with one missing

HEAD CHARACTERISTICS:
Fairly flat profile to head;
small leather patch nose

BODY CHARACTERISTICS:
Round body; short arms; pointed feet,
pads repaired with brown vinyl

DISTINGUISHING FEATURES:
Split above left eye; one ear missing
and left arm stitched to body;
green ribbon around neck.

—JOHNNY BEAR—

Public Collection. Courtesy of the Museum of the City of New York, New York, the United States.

JOHNNY BEAR was made in 1905 and is a favourite at the Museum of the City of New York in the United States, where all the beautiful antique toys on display have been donated to the museum by residents of the city.

Johnny was named by his original owner, Mildred Irving, later Mrs Gordon Turner, who was born in New York at the turn of the century. The photograph, taken in 1905, shows Mildred aged five sitting with her favourite companion, Johnny Bear, who was then new and fluffy. Johnny eventually became quite bald as his fur was slowly loved away and nowadays the bear's striking profile is nothing like that of the old photograph.

According to the bear's original family Johnny once owned an extensive wardrobe and the dashing native

Mildred Irving, Johnny Bear's owner, aged five, with Johnny Bear (1905)

American outfit he wears today, which once featured a matching headdress, is one of these original costumes. The worn areas on Johnny Bear's feet have been patched many times with beige fabric and give the illusion he is wearing a pair of native American moccasins.

The Museum of the City of New York is adjacent to Central Park and children from local schools are encouraged to visit the delightful collection. Children receive fun questionnaires about the exhibits which are designed to make their visit even more enjoyable and ensure their interest in the future of this fascinating museum.

On the opposite page, Johnny is pictured seated on a lovely old wooden drum, circa 1875, which was donated by another New Yorker, Edmund Bramhall Child. From this elevated position the all American Johnny Bear can peer down his extraordinary nose at almost everyone.

THE BEAR ESSENTIALS – JOHNNY BEAR

DATE OF BIRTH:
1905 made in the United States, possibly by the Ideal Toy Company

HEIGHT:
16 in or 41 cm

FUR TYPE:
Golden coloured mohair, worn.

FILLING:
Excelsior/wood-wool.

EYES AND EARS:
Clear glass eyes, original; large ears set in unusual position, well towards the side of head

HEAD CHARACTERISTICS:
Pointed snout; fur very worn on head; nose stitching worn

BODY CHARACTERISTICS:
Small hump on back; long arms with thin curved paws; paws repaired with pale beige cotton fabric; claw stitching missing; feet repaired with layers of beige fabric

DISTINGUISHING FEATURES:
Original handmade native American-style clothes

—LITTLE RED—

Private Collection. Courtesy of the Owner.

HAPPY MEMORIES of childhood include such wonders as Father Christmas, the Tooth Fairy and the Easter Bunny, but for his young owner the magical appearance of this teddy bear, named Little Red, was unsurpassed.

In an English coastal town during the 1950s the owner of this bear, then a five-year-old child, was taken by her parents to visit a magic wishing well and was overheard wishing fervently and loudly for "A little teddy bear please, with red clothes…".

The earnest plea brought a smile to her parents' faces and amused the passers-by. The child waited patiently for a teddy bear to leap from the depths of the magic well and was understandably disappointed when her parents led her home before the miracle could occur.

One day soon after, she awoke to find a little golden teddy bear tucked beneath her pillow and, joy of joys, he was dressed in a bright red knitted suit.

The pure elation of such a find was never forgotten by the child who saw the bear, which she named Little Red, as tangible proof of the powers of magic.

Much loved, Little Red eventually grew quite bald and the wool in his knitted suit slowly unravelled and was lost. Now, many years later, Little Red still lives with his original owner and has been comfortably rehoused in an old velvet evening bag, wrapped warmly in a spotted silk scarf.

THE BEAR ESSENTIALS – LITTLE RED

DATE OF BIRTH:
1950 probably made in Japan

HEIGHT:
6 in or 15 cm

FUR TYPE:
Gold coloured cotton plush

FILLING:
Excelsior/wood-wool

HEAD CHARACTERISTICS:
Small glass eyes; restitched nose and mouth

BODY CHARACTERISTICS:
Simple construction; head and body in one piece;
Limbs articulated with wire rods

DISTINGUISHING FEATURES:
Little Red's restitched mouth is bright red wool,
a scrap of wool from his original knitted suit

LITTLE TOMMY TITTLEMOUSE

Public Collection. By courtesy of the Board of the Trustees of the Victoria and Albert Museum, London, England.

THERE IS nothing more Little Tommy Tittlemouse prefers to do on a cold, wet afternoon, than sort through his letter collection.

Little Tommy Tittlemouse was given his unusual name by his original owner, James Gower, who was born in Iver, Buckinghamshire, England in 1907. The teddy bear was a gift for James' first birthday.

Much loved, Little Tommy Tittlemouse was greatly treasured and the stuffing in the little bear's arms became loose where James constantly held him. Eventually the teddy became almost bald, however, this kind of wear is not consistent with rough handling, simply years of gentle cuddling.

In 1965 James Gower donated Little Tommy Tittlemouse to the Bethnal Green Museum of Childhood but continued to visit his bear and never failed to send him a card or letter on his birthday.

Also pictured are three bears who all belonged to Mrs M.P. Drewitt who owned the teddies as a child in Italy in 1910. The dark brown bear on the left was

74

originally a pull-along toy and the holes in his paws show where he was once attached to a little platform on wheels. The fat bear on the right of the group is called Orsetto (which means little bear in Italian) and accompanied his young owner on many travels. Once during a long journey, Orsetto went missing and, in an attempt to pacify the distressed child, her aunt bought her the small bear with the yellow ribbon seated in the centre of the group. Fortunately, Orsetto was later found, and the three bears lived happily ever after.

THE BEAR ESSENTIALS – LITTLE TOMMY TITTLEMOUSE

DATE OF BIRTH:
1908 made in Germany

HEIGHT:
7 in or 18 cm

FUR TYPE:
Golden coloured mohair plush, very worn condition

FILLING:
Excelsior/wood-wool

EYES AND EARS:
Original black boot-button type eyes; prominent round ears

HEAD CHARACTERISTICS:
Pronounced snout, nose stitching very worn

BODY CHARACTERISTICS:
Small hump on back; squeaker in body (now inoperative); long straight arms; no paw pads; large feet; foot pads repaired with leather; remains of claw stitching evident

DISTINGUISHING FEATURES:
Little Tommy Tittlemouse is almost completely bald except for a few tufts of hair in his seams; the excelsior stuffing in his arms has been displaced as the result of being held constantly

As for Little Tommy Tittlemouse, it is a sad fact that many bears outlive their owners. James Gower died in 1986 and, every year since then, Little Tommy Tittlemouse has waited in vain for his birthday card. But he keeps cheerful, for no-one can take away his happy memories and, of course, he still has his letters!

"Send me a letter, send me a card,
A telegram or a note,
Say that you love me, say that you care
It's ages since you wrote."

—LONDON TOY AND MODEL MUSEUM—

Public Collection. Courtesy of The London Toy and Model Museum, London, England.

A VISIT TO the London Toy and Model Museum is always a treat. The award-winning museum holds an extensive collection of toys which is housed in two large mid-Victorian buildings which are a five minute walk from historic Paddington Station.

Inside the museum, toy trains, cars, aeroplanes, dolls and teddy bears are all there to be enjoyed. Outside, you can walk in the garden where steam and electric trains run alongside a children's carousel. You can also enjoy the delicious ice cream served at the museum's cafe.

The late actor Peter Bull, an unabashed pioneer of teddy bear lovers and one-time owner of the famous Delicatessen (the bear who played Aloysius in the television series *Brideshead Revisited*), organised annual teddy bear picnics in the museum's gardens. He also bequeathed his famous teddy bear collection to the museum. Most of the bears in the museum can be found in the Edwardian nursery, a room styled to look like a giant doll's house. Arranged around the original cast-iron kitchen range are teddy bears reading books, taking tea, and reclining on rocking chairs. Two aviator bears hang precariously overhead in a wooden aeroplane.

Sitting quietly amidst all the activity is an old Steiff bear known as the Smiling Bear and his pal, a little bear from the early 1900s. A red Pierrot doll, a fairground souvenir from the 1930s, swings happily above the pair.

These musical pigs are also part of the Musem's collection

The Smiling Bear is a London Toy and Model Museum favourite who often features in the museum's promotional material. The most contented of bears, quite simply the smile on his face says it all.

In 1994, The London Toy and Model Museum underwent extensive refurbishment, which included the installation of 23 new themed galleries fitted with sounds and smells to create authentic atmospheres. New audiovisual displays and a special hands-on education room have also been included.

THE BEAR ESSENTIALS – SMILING BEAR

DATE OF BIRTH:
1907 probably made in Germany by Steiff

HEIGHT:
17 in or 44 cm

FUR TYPE:
Golden coloured mohair, very worn condition

FILLING:
Excelsior/wood-wool

EYES AND EARS:
Round, black, boot-button eyes, original; ears set across head seams; metal button in ear, trademark of Steiff company

HEAD CHARACTERISTICS:
Pronounced snout, nose stitching worn; original mouth stitching missing; replacement 'smile' added

BODY CHARACTERISTICS:
Large feet with original felt pads, worn in places

DISTINGUISHING FEATURES:
Worn areas on snout and an unmistakable smile

—Melissa's Bear—

Courtesy of Melissa, Melbourne, Victoria, Australia.

AS A DIRECT result of his immense appeal this little bear escaped being given away as a birthday present and now lives happily with Melissa.

In 1989 Melissa travelled overseas. As her friend Mark was soon to celebrate his 21st birthday in Australia, Melissa visited the famous Harrods store in London to search for the perfect present. The series *Brideshead Revisited* had recently been televised and Melissa knew how much Mark had enjoyed the program so, when she saw a teddy bear replica of Delicatessen (the bear who had played Aloysius in the series) she knew it would make the ideal gift. The original Delicatessen was a bear so named because he had spent many years on a shelf in an American grocery store before being given to the late British actor and lover of teddy bears, Peter Bull. As an actor, Peter Bull immediately noticed Delicatessen's star potential and auditioned the bear for the part of Aloysius in the *Brideshead Revisited* series. Delicatessen became an overnight success and never looked back. He now lives comfortably in the United States and there are 5000 small replicas of him scattered all around the world.

By carefully copying the original bear the Delicatessen replicas were manufactured to look extremely world weary. Made from 'distressed' mohair plush, the replica bears had chamois leather patches all over their bodies in exactly the same places as their namesake. Each Delicatessen replica also had a small British Airways flight bag to travel in and wore a Daks Simpson scarf.

The bear left Harrods with Melissa and accompanied her on her travels around Europe and the United States. They met lots of new friends, flew on Concorde together and stayed at the best hotels. So it really comes as no surprise that, as she sadly tucked him into his small travel bag for the flight home to Australia,

Melissa realised she simply could not part with him. Back in Australia Melissa bought Mark another handsome teddy bear and dressed him in a flying suit, complete with helmet and goggles. She presented this bear to Mark on his 21st birthday and he was delighted. Later, with considerable honesty, Melissa confessed how she had fallen in love with the other little bear and Mark, as a fellow arctophile, entirely understood her dilemma.

THE BEAR ESSENTIALS — MELISSA'S BEAR

DATE OF BIRTH:
1988 made in England
by House of Nisbet,
replica of Delicatessen

HEIGHT:
14 in or 36 cm

FUR TYPE:
Pale golden colour,
'distressed' mohair

FILLING:
Excelsior/wood-wool

EYES AND EARS:
Black plastic button eyes

HEAD CHARACTERISTICS:
Triangular-shaped head;
wide stitched nose with small piece
of red felt stitched below

BODY CHARACTERISTICS:
Rounded body; long arms;
paws and one foot pad
in matching beige fabric
remaining left foot pad
in pink felt with House of Nisbet
label stitched on; small leather
patches sewn over bear's body
to replicate those of the original
Delicatessen bear

DISTINGUISHING FEATURES:
Label sewn into side seam
which reads
"World Edition of 5000,
this is Number 2567"

— THE MERCHANTS' HOUSE BEARS —

Public collection. Courtesy of the Merchants' House, Sydney, Australia. Grateful thanks to Robert Holden, Sydney, New South Wales, Australia.

THE MERCHANTS' House, situated in The Rocks, Sydney, houses the National Trust Australian Childhood Collection — a fascinating selection of Australian toys which date from early colonial times to present day.

In a corner sit two old teddy bears from the 1940s mesmerised by a jack-in-the-box. The little bear with the pink ribbon has his owner's name stitched across his chest. Mothers often labelled their children's toys in this manner to soothe anxious children when teddy was lost and it is obvious that little Judy-Gaye Greening did not wish to lose her bear. Although the larger bear is missing both eyes his expression shows that the old jack-in-the-box has surprised him. The jack-in-the-box, circa 1930s, is a product of ingenuity, constructed as it is from an old bed spring, a painted cotton reel and lots of imagination.

Ready for take-off in a homemade toy aeroplane circa 1930s is Robert Holden's teddy bear. Robert and Richard Holden are identical twins who were born in 1948. The boys were given identical Australian-made Joy Toys teddy bears at their christening, which proved to be a riotous family occasion. As the parents-to-be were

Robert and Richard Holden,
identical twins
who owned identical bears
(circa early 1950s)

jack-in the-box were quite acceptable.

Ingenuity was what counted and the

endless imagination of a child made everything possible.

not anticipating

twins it was a time

of great celebration.

Robert and Richard

had no distinguishing

marks and, at the

christening, their parents were

still relying on the hospital name tags attached to the babies'

wrists. The merriment and drink flowed freely and somehow

during the celebration the babies' name tags came off. To this

day, neither of the boys can be quite sure if he is really Robert

or Richard. As an adult Robert Holden played an important

role in establishing the National Trust Childhood Collection,

located in Sydney.

There is a charm and naiveté about the toys in this

collection which is hard to describe. Perhaps a reminder of a

time when children had unsophisticated tastes and an

aeroplane with wheels from mum's old pram, or a home-made

THE BEAR ESSENTIALS –

BEAR WITH PINK RIBBON

DATE OF BIRTH:
Circa 1940 made in Australia, probably by Verna

HEIGHT:
16 in or 42 cm

FUR TYPE:
Long golden coloured mohair, worn condition

FILLING:
Soft filled

EYES AND EARS:
Ears set over side seams of head

HEAD CHARACTERISTICS:
Wedge-shaped muzzle, characteristic of Verna bears; nose stitching missing; amber glass eyes original

BODY CHARACTERISTICS:
Original rexine pads, worn

DISTINGUISHING FEATURES:
School name label ("Judy-Gaye Greening") stitched to bear's front

LARGE BEAR

DATE OF BIRTH:
Circa 1940 made in Australia, probably by Verna

HEIGHT:
23 in or 60 cm

FUR TYPE:
Golden coloured mohair

EYES AND EARS:
The bear has lost both eyes

HEAD CHARACTERISTICS:
The bear has lost most of his nose and mouth

BODY CHARACTERISTICS:
Still has three original rexine pads, one foot has been repaired with checked silk fabric

—Mister Bear—

Private collection. Courtesy of the Owner, Melbourne, Victoria, Australia.

MISTER BEAR was given to Joy Lewis in 1926, for her 11th birthday. Joy was the youngest of four sisters and, as a little girl, she had desperately wanted a big brother. Her childhood imagination solved the problem when Mister Bear arrived and he soon came to represent the brother Joy had yearned for.

Joy and Mister Bear were inseparable. Newspaper cuttings from 1929 show Joy as a schoolgirl holding Mister Bear, dressed in his own St. Michael's uniform, as they cheered the school at their annual sports day. Childhood years passed and Joy married a sea captain. As a naval wife she spent long periods of time alone while her husband was at sea and Mister Bear became her defence against loneliness. As Joy recalls "he became not a bear, but almost a person to me". Indeed Mister Bear was always there, in good times and bad when he would loan Joy his nose to cry on.

Mister Bear has attended numerous parties and celebrations and was even featured in an article about teddy bears in *The Herald and Weekly Times* newspaper.

Joy is well known for her delightful sense of humour and each year she celebrates her birthday with Mister Bear. Joy's friends share the joke and address all her cards and presents to Mister Bear. The advantage of this practice is that it is Mister Bear, not Joy, who ages another year.

Mister Bear is filled with an unusual combination of cork granules and wood-wool but his exciting lifestyle and the increasing years have taken their toll so, for his 50th birthday, Mister Bear received a tailor-made velvet suit which had the cuffs and trouser ends stitched up to prevent his cork filling escaping. Mister Bear's head has been

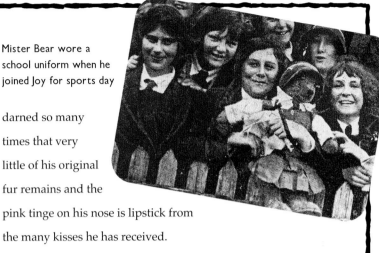

Mister Bear wore a school uniform when he joined Joy for sports day

darned so many times that very little of his original fur remains and the pink tinge on his nose is lipstick from the many kisses he has received.

Much loved Mister Bear continues to keep a kindly eye on his owner and, as Joy says "With Mister Bear I have never really been alone".

THE BEAR ESSENTIALS – MISTER BEAR

DATE OF BIRTH:
1926 made in England

HEIGHT:
30 in or 76 cm

FUR TYPE:
Originally golden coloured mohair, extremely worn condition

FILLING:
Head filled with cork granules, body filled with excelsior/wood-wool

EYES AND EARS:
Clear glass eyes original, left eye cracked; large ears, set below side seam on head

HEAD CHARACTERISTICS:
Bear's head completely covered in repair stitches, head filled with cork granules; nose and mouth restitched

BODY CHARACTERISTICS:
Pronounced hump on back; tip growler mechanism still in operation

DISTINGUISHING FEATURES:
Bear's head and body extensively repaired; nose stained with lipstick, Mr. Bear is unmistakable

—Orange Ribbon Bear—

Private Collection. Courtesy of the Owner, Australia.

THIS LOVELY brown bear was brought into an antique shop by an elderly lady who told the dealer that the bear must find a new home with a caring owner, preferably someone with a "kind face". The old bear had belonged to her late husband, who had been given the toy as a child in 1908. The elderly lady had looked after the bear ever since her husband's death, however, as her own health was failing she wished to ensure the bear was settled into a comfortable new home.

The old teddy bear was made of dark brown woollen cloth and his body was filled with an unusual mix of fine cork granules. The bear's lead weight growler still rattled inside him and he wore his original blue and white striped suit, which had been carefully hand-sewn and secured down the back with rows of old-fashioned metal fastenings.

Before leaving her husband's bear in the antique store, the elderly lady requested that the new owner never remove the orange ribbon that was tied around the teddy bear's leg. The ribbon had been there for as long as she could recall and had held particular significance for her late husband who had never untied it.

THE BEAR ESSENTIALS — ORANGE RIBBON BEAR

DATE OF BIRTH:
1908

HEIGHT:
15 in or 37 cm

FUR TYPE:
Dark brown woollen fabric

FILLING:
Cork granules

EYES AND EARS:
Round black boot-button eyes; small rounded ears set into head and across side seams

HEAD CHARACTERISTICS:
Fairly flat face; horizontal stitched nose of black wool

BODY CHARACTERISTICS:
Slight hump on back; long arms and large feet, original beige felt paws, patched, with five claws on paws, four claws on feet

DISTINGUISHING FEATURES:
The bear's orange ribbon, tied securely to right ankle and tan woollen repair stitch work below right eye

Her failing memory could not assist with any further details and the poignant story of the bear and his ribbon is now lost in time.

Orange Ribbon Bear now lives happily with his new owner. The scrap of ribbon remains tied and perhaps only the bear knows the reason it is there and it seems he certainly knows how to keep a secret!

—PILCHARD—

Private Collection. Courtesy of the Owner, Victoria, Australia.

The brim of the hat was lavishly decorated with heavy silk flowers and as Pilchard peered out from beneath the petals his future owner was won over by the bear's demure expression. Ever a bear of contrasts, Pilchard was also wearing a stout, practical, brown leather collar.

The lure of a teddy bear is strong and his current owner left a deposit and took him home a few weeks later. Soon after, Pilchard's new owner, a collector of Victorian jewellery and accessories, took him along to an antique fair to model some necklaces.

It was a busy morning and Pilchard was patted and admired by many customers. He also helped his owner sell several pieces. Then, to everyone's horror, it was noticed that Pilchard had disappeared from his chair.

An urgent message — that a teddy bear, wearing a pearl necklace, had gone missing — was put out over the loudspeakers. The exit doors of the venue were locked by security guards and an extensive search took place.

Fortunately for Pilchard the thief panicked and the distraught bear was located in a waste paper bin with his pearl necklace intact.

PILCHARD is a mystery bear who owes his unusual name to his bright orange fur which has been compared to the colour of tinned pilchards.

Pilchard was found sitting in an old pram several years ago. He was trying to wear an outsize Victorian hat but, as his owner recalls, the hat actually appeared to be wearing him.

None the worse for his adventure, Pilchard still attends the occasional antique fair but nowadays he confines himself to modelling hats and always has his paw tied firmly to a chair.

THE BEAR ESSENTIALS – PILCHARD

DATE OF BIRTH:
Circa 1940 probably made in Australia

HEIGHT:
19 in or 48 cm

FUR TYPE:
Bright orange cotton plush

FILLING:
Kapok

EYES AND EARS:
Original clear glass eyes; ears set below side seams and inserted into head

HEAD CHARACTERISTICS:
Head and body in one piece; fairly short muzzle; vertical stitched nose with extended outside stitches

BODY CHARACTERISTICS:
Short curved arms; shaped legs; original pads, brown rexine with marbled pattern

DISTINGUISHING FEATURES:
Rexine on paws cracked; repair work on underside of legs; Pilchard always wears a flamboyant hat

—Pillow—

Private Collection. Courtesy K. and S. Philips, Berkshire, England.

A TEDDY BEAR is understandably a very difficult toy to share.

Pillow Bear was bought for twins Kate and Sarah by their aunt circa 1940. Both little girls adored him and, as a result, the bear became the subject of a long, drawn out custody battle.

Kate and Sarah recall having many heated arguments over Pillow.

Their mother, in an effort to keep the peace between the girls, made a roster as to which twin should take the bear to bed each night. However, sleeping without the bear seemed impossible and, as often as not, the twin deprived of Pillow's company for the night would creep across and recapture the bear from her sister's bed. In this way the arguments over Pillow often continued well into the night.

Pillow's neat little body once had delicately shaped paws but because of the furious battles he was involved in his arms are now very loose and he is completely bald save for a few tufts of fur on his seams.

As the twins grew older they certainly grew wiser. An agreement was struck and Sarah, the elder twin and now a landscape designer, has custody of Pillow while her sister Kate has full visiting rights.

Peace at last for Pillow. The bear has a warm spot on Sarah's windowsill where he sits amongst her cyclamens and happily watches the garden grow.

THE BEAR ESSENTIALS — PILLOW

DATE OF BIRTH:
1940 made in England

HEIGHT:
12 in or 30 cm

FUR TYPE:
Golden coloured mohair, very worn.

FILLING:
Excelsior/wood-wool in head, soft fill in body

EYES AND EARS:
Glass eyes, original; small ears inserted below side seam of head

HEAD CHARACTERISTICS:
Small head, dart seams across head into which ears are inserted; original nose, vertical stitching

BODY CHARACTERISTICS:
Thin curved arms; straight legs very little foot shaping, original rexine pads on paws; push squeaker in body not in operation

DISTINGUISHING FEATURES:
Very little fur and extremely loose arms; blue woollen trousers

—PLUMMY—

Courtesy of Judy and John Sparrow, The Bear Museum, Petersfield, Hants, England.

Browsing through most contemporary design magazines it soon becomes clear that, despite modern styling, we love nostalgia. Rustic, country-style and 'distressed' furniture and accessories are back in fashion and so is Plummy Bear whose simplicity is a pure delight.

Plummy Bear was made for Judy Sparrow and her sister during 1943 in England when, due to wartime evacuation, the little girls were staying with their grandmother and aunt. The pair were given Plummy by a distant, elderly relative who ran a nearby public house. She had acquired the bear from one of her customers who was a retired dressmaker and, as materials were in short supply, Plummy had been fashioned from an old camel hair coat.

It has to be said that Plummy was not an immediate success with the little girls. With typical childlike honesty they noticed that Plummy was "not furry"

like their other bears Newie and Oldie. In fact, due to Plummy's huge ears and unusual shape, they were not entirely convinced he was even a teddy bear. Judy named him Plummy due to his small round glass eyes which

Judy, right, holding Plummmy and Oldie.
Her sister, left, holds Newie
(circa 1940s)

resembled currants in a plum pudding. In 1948, after the war had ended, the girls moved back to their own home. In all the excitement that followed the girls forgot about their homemade bear and poor old Plummy was left behind.

Fortunately for the little bear Judy's aunt had a small collection of soft toys and, as the years passed, when it became clear that Plummy had been abandoned their aunt grew very fond of him. She dressed him in a white baby's gown and he sat in her bedroom until 1985 when, as an elderly lady, she was taken into care. As the old house was cleared, long lost Plummy was rediscovered and Judy, now a respected collector, author and restorer of teddy bears, viewed Plummy in an entirely new light. With a new found appreciation for the old bear, Judy took him home and he now lives at The Bear Museum in Petersfield.

THE BEAR ESSENTIALS – PLUMMY

DATE OF BIRTH:
1943, homemade toy

HEIGHT:
15 in or 38 cm tall

FUR TYPE:
Recycled camel hair fabric

FILLING:
Kapok

EYES AND EARS:
Small, round, brown glass eyes
sewn deeply into head;
very large rounded ears

HEAD CHARACTERISTICS:
Rounded head, with slight shaping
to profile; nose a piece of beige
felt, stitched on; black wool mouth
secured in place with beige thread.

BODY CHARACTERISTICS:
Uncomplicated design; round body
shape with dart halfway down
centre-front; slight shaping to
arms and legs; paws and pads are
circles of recycled tan leather.
Body jointed in crude manner
with thread and leather
reinforcing circles
on the outside of his limbs

**DISTINGUISHING
FEATURES:**
Plummy's unusual shape
and construction make
him quite unique

—POLLOCK'S TOY MUSEUM—

Public Collection. Courtesy of Pollock's Toy Museum, London, England.

POLLOCK'S Toy Museum is situated in an evocative 18th century building in West London. The bears live on the top floor and look perfectly at home in the subdued lighting of the old house.

Sitting quietly side-by-side in a corner are William, a teddy bear from 1908 and Freda, an old doll with a bisque head and leather body. The pair arrived at the museum together and their poignant card states 'Freda and William — never parted'. Across the room an old bear from 1914 stoically holds the Union Jack. He is dressed in First World War uniform, complete with tin hat and whistle. Influenced by the Great War his original owner, a child named Helen Roy

Lister, made her bear several uniforms. Beside him sits Eric, who wears an extraordinary black velvet suit. Eric has a label around his neck which claims he is "The Oldest Known Teddy Bear" a fact no-one would dare dispute, at least not within earshot of Eric. Now in his twilight years, Eric is a little loose of limb but has lost none of his patriotic fervour and, as the Union Jack flies above, of course "There'll always be an England".

THE BEAR ESSENTIALS –
SOLDIER BEAR

DATE OF BIRTH:
Circa 1909

HEIGHT:
13 in or 33cm

FUR TYPE:
Gold coloured mohair plush

EYES AND EARS:
Black boot-button eyes

BODY
CHARACTERISTICS:
Long limbs; small hump
on back

DISTINGUISHING
FEATURES:
Soldier Bear has several
uniforms which can be seen
at the museum

WILLIAM

DATE OF BIRTH:
Circa 1908

HEIGHT:
17 in or 43cm

FUR TYPE:
Light golden coloured mohair

FILLING:
Excelsior/wood-wool

HEAD
CHARACTERISTICS:
Has a shaved muzzle

BODY
CHARACTERISTICS:
Long limbs and original
felt paw pads

ERIC

DATE OF BIRTH:
Circa 1905

HEIGHT:
12 in or 30 cm

FUR TYPE:
Golden coloured mohair

FILLING:
Excelsior/wood-wool

HEAD
CHARACTERISTICS:
Black boot-button eyes

BODY
CHARACTERISTICS:
Long limbs and a small
hump on his back

FREDA AND WILLIAM
(NEVER PARTED)

—POWERHOUSE TOYS—

Courtesy of The Powerhouse Museum, Sydney, New South Wales, Australia.

REGARDED AS the finest museum of its type in Australia, the Powerhouse is a spectacular building on the western side of Darling Harbour in Sydney, Australia. The Powerhouse contains some fascinating collections and places emphasis on 'hands-on' educational activities for children.

Held in the museum's extensive collection are two little dolls dressed in their pyjamas. They once belonged to the Peters family in Germany. Sasha, the boy doll, was given to six year old Toni Peters for Christmas in 1924 and the girl doll, Ursula, arrived in 1930. Both dolls were made an extensive wardrobe by Toni's mother, Anna Peters. Their clothes provide an interesting reflection of fashion at the time, as some of their outfits were actual copies of garments worn by the Peters family.

Nearby, some Australian toys sit with an English teddy bear who was sent to a little Australian girl named Kimberley in the 1950s. Some 40 years later she still recalls the great excitement she felt when the large box containing Teddy arrived from overseas. Teddy wears his original handknitted jumper and often visits the Powerhouse toy collection where Kimberley is a curator. The kangaroo, named Jacko, was made by Amy Raymond in 1907 for her small daughter Mildred. Amy made Jacko from odd scraps of material and his well worn paws and chewed nose make him a charming example of a much loved homemade toy.

The stuffed leopard reclines quietly and surveys the scene with his one remaining green glass eye. The leopard, named Spots, belonged to Dame Nancy Bird, one of Australia's first women pilots. Spots was her mascot and accompanied her on many trips aboard her De Havilland Leopard Moth Aircraft in the 1930s.

Although the Powerhouse toys have varied histories they have one thing in common — all were greatly treasured by their original owners.

THE BEAR ESSENTIALS – KIMBERLEY'S BEAR

DATE OF BIRTH:
Circa 1950 made
in England

HEIGHT:
16 in or 40 cm

FILLING:
Synthetic fibre

EYES AND EARS:
Orange plastic eyes;
small, well spaced ears

HEAD CHARACTERISTICS:
Fairly broad head;
vertical stitched nose,
damaged

BODY CHARACTERISTICS:
Typical English-style teddy bear
of the period; short arms
and straight legs
with velvet pads, original

DISTINGUISHING FEATURES:
Worn nose stitching;
wears original knitted clothes
from the 1950s

THE DOLL ESSENTIALS

DATE OF BIRTH:
Sasha circa 1924, Ursula circa
1930. Both made in Germany
by doll manufacturer Kathe
Kruse

HEIGHT:
Sasha 17 in or 43 cm
Ursula 19 in or 50 cm

HEAD CHARACTERISTICS:
Face handmade with gauze and
plaster, all features hand-
painted

BODY CHARACTERISTICS:
Complicated seam construction
from head to body, stuffed
with horse hair

DISTINGUISHING FEATURES:
Each has an extensive
hand-sewn wardrobe

THE KANGAROO ESSENTIALS – JACKO

DATE OF BIRTH:
1907, homemade toy

FILLING:
Excelsior/wood-wool

EYES AND EARS:
Glass button eyes

BODY CHARACTERISTICS:
Made from various cotton fabrics
with velvet inserts, legs and
forearms made from black
material, fawn body, brown tail
and caramel coloured stomach
and pouch, nose and mouth
stitched from black cotton

THE LEOPARD ESSENTIALS – SPOTS

DATE OF BIRTH:
Circa 1930s

LENGTH:
16 in or 40 cm

FUR TYPE:
Artificial leopard skin plush

FILLING:
Fibre stuffing

EYES AND EARS:
Green glass eyes, one missing

—Richard's Rabbit—

Private collection. Courtesy of the Owner, London, England.

Richard with his rabbit
(circa 1940s)

IT MAY SEEM strange that a rabbit should find its way into the pages of a teddy bear book. However, for many years, as the result of a case of mistaken identity, Richard believed his rabbit was in fact a teddy bear.

It was not until a friend pointed out that teddy bears were furry and did not have long green ears that the awful truth was realised. Nevertheless, the rabbit acquitted himself admirably and fulfilled the role of a good bear during some hectic wartime years when teddies were in short supply.

In 1944 London was being bombed nightly and air raid sirens would warn the population when a bombing raid was imminent. Richard, a baby at the time, would be wrapped in a blanket with his rabbit and raced to an underground shelter for safety. Many nights were spent anxiously waiting for danger to pass and the little knitted rabbit was a great comfort.

The rabbit was given to Richard by his Aunt Hilda who purchased it from a London bazaar held to assist the Second World War effort. Throughout the war materials were in short supply and children's toys depended on the ingenuity of their parents. Magazines of the day published patterns to meet the demand for homemade toys and, as knitting wool was rationed, old woollen garments were recycled and knitted into soft toys. Richard's rabbit is a perfect example of such work. Knitted in an assortment of green, beige and pink wools, he was stuffed with scraps of old rayon stockings, his ears were lined with an oddment of green twill and two large rabbit eyes were cut from a scrap of green felt.

As the years passed the faithful rabbit endured many a rough game at the hands of Richard and his siblings. His knitted arms stretched longer and longer and his striped woollen body grew patched and faded. Richard grew up and became a prominent architect and the little green rabbit, who was once a teddy bear, stayed with his family.

THE RABBIT DETAILS – RICHARD'S RABBIT

DATE OF BIRTH:
1944, homemade toy

HEIGHT:
14 in or 35 cm, including ears

FUR TYPE:
Assortment of knitting wools

FILLING:
Recycled scraps of rayon stockings

EYES AND EARS:
Eyes cut from two oval pieces of thick felt, "pupil" stitched in black silk, ears lined with twill fabric

HEAD CHARACTERISTICS:
Oval knitted shape, mouth stitched in red wool

BODY CHARACTERISTICS:
Simple knitted construction, not articulated

DISTINGUISHING FEATURES:
Repair in centre of body; long stretched arms

—Rippon Lea Bear—

Public Collection. Gift of Mrs Aitkin to Rippon Lea, Melbourne, Victoria, Australia, in 1985. Model for drawing by courtesy of The National Trust of Australia.

RIPPON LEA Bear, circa 1916, is a handsome old bear who spends his retirement being admired by the many visitors to Rippon Lea, a beautiful National Trust house and estate in Melbourne, Victoria, Australia. Rippon Lea was built by Sir Frederick Sargood during the late 19th century, a prosperous and optimistic period for the city often described as "Marvellous Melbourne". Sir Frederick Sargood was a successful businessman with a large family and Rippon Lea became the Sargood family home. A keen gardener, Sir Frederick was personally involved in the planning and design of his 43 acres of grounds which provided his children and their friends with a magical environment in which to play. The grounds boast a lookout tower nestled high amongst the trees, a lake complete with small rowing boats as well as numerous secret paths and hiding places which would have provided hours of amusement for the Sargood children.

The original owners of Rippon Lea, the Sargood family, shown here playing tennis (1888)
(Reproduced by kind permission of Brian Webster.)

Opposite page: This cheeky fellow is also part of the Rippon Lea collection

Upstairs in the house a children's nursery has been recreated and features a fine collection of antique toys. Seated in an old pram amongst the dolls, soldiers and rocking horse is the Rippon Lea Bear. This grand old bear dominates the nursery and, with his imperious nose held high in the air and stern downturned mouth, it appears he has finally found a position which suits his importance.

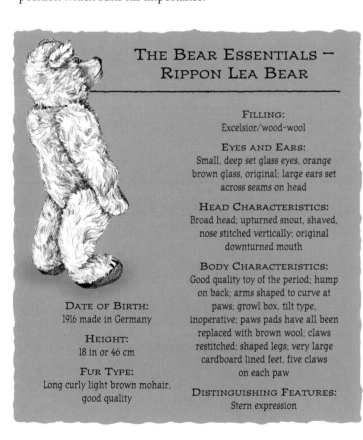

THE BEAR ESSENTIALS – RIPPON LEA BEAR

DATE OF BIRTH:
1916 made in Germany

HEIGHT:
18 in or 46 cm

FUR TYPE:
Long curly light brown mohair, good quality

FILLING:
Excelsior/wood-wool

EYES AND EARS:
Small, deep set glass eyes, orange brown glass, original; large ears set across seams on head

HEAD CHARACTERISTICS:
Broad head; upturned snout, shaved, nose stitched vertically; original downturned mouth

BODY CHARACTERISTICS:
Good quality toy of the period; hump on back; arms shaped to curve at paws; growl box, tilt type, inoperative; paws pads have all been replaced with brown wool; claws restitched; shaped legs; very large cardboard lined feet, five claws on each paw

DISTINGUISHING FEATURES:
Stern expression

—Robin's Bear—

Courtesy of Robin, Melbourne, Victoria, Australia.

ROBIN IS blessed with a warm, sunny personality and her interesting antique shop, called Robin Hood, attracts a wide range of collectors and customers alike, many of whom pop in just for the opportunity to chat with Robin.

Robin's shop specialises in antique brass beds which she displays with great flair.

Always on the lookout for bits and pieces to accessorise her stock, Robin rescued this old teddy bear many years ago from beneath a pile of second-hand clothes in a Salvation Army shop. Despite his sad expression and well worn paws, Robin took the bear back to her shop where she found him a little pair of socks and tucked him up inside a Victorian baby's cot. He looked so comfortable that many of her customers offered to buy him and the teddy bear soon began to wear a 'NOT FOR SALE' sign.

The bear's fur cleaned up to a bright golden colour and it was revealed that he was a fine example of an Australian-made Joy Toys teddy bear. In 1989 Robin was asked if the bear could represent Australia in a toy exhibition. She agreed and placed the bear behind a curtain at the back of the shop to await his collection the following day. That night, thieves broke into the shop and many valuable items were stolen including antique dolls and other bears from the showcases. Peering out from the shadows, well hidden behind the heavy red curtain, this fortunate bear escaped capture by the thieves.

If only bears could talk, what a help he could have been to the police, especially as he was wearing his large watch and chain and would have known the exact time of the robbery.

Robin, the bear's owner
(circa 1940s)

THE BEAR ESSENTIALS — ROBIN'S BEAR

DATE OF BIRTH:
1930–40s made in Australia by Joy Toys

HEIGHT:
30 in or 76 cm

FUR TYPE:
Bright golden coloured mohair in good condition

FILLING:
Excelsior/wood-wool

EYES AND EARS:
Large brown glass eyes

HEAD CHARACTERISTICS:
Well spaced large ears; round head; black nose with extended stitch either side, characteristic of Joy Toys bears

BODY CHARACTERISTICS:
Round body; fairly short arms with upturned paws

DISTINGUISHING FEATURES:
Foot pads very worn on feet; excelsior stuffing evident

—THE ROGERS FAMILY BEAR—

Private collection. With grateful thanks to Robin Kelly and the Rogers family in Melbourne, Victoria, Australia

George Rogers with his bear
(circa 1920s)

THIS BEAUTIFUL wheeled bear once belonged to Dorothy Rogers and her family. Dorothy was a writer and a collection of her poems and children's verse was published in London in 1932. She was also an historian and used her extensive knowledge of the Kew district to write the book *A History of Kew* which was published in 1972.

The wheeled bear was bought for George, the eldest Rogers boy, in the 1920s. The bear soon became a great favourite with all the Rogers family. Watching her three lively sons, George, John and David, playing on the old wheeled bear obviously provided her with the inspiration to write the poem *My Bear*, which can be found opposite the title page of this book.

John later recalled, "When children were riding on his back, the Bear had a tendency to tip onto his nose if he ran into any small object on the floor, which usually resulted in the child doing the same. He was certainly a favourite with my brothers and me, as well as lots of cousins and friends who came to visit our home. He also survived the assault of Dorothy's seven grandchildren which explains why the poor old thing looks so worn".

As a result of all the rides he had given the bear's back eventually grew bald, so a blue felt saddle was carefully stitched to his back. A red felt collar was also attached to strengthen his wobbly neck joint.

In 1973 the Dorothy Rogers Reserve was opened at Kew Junction in Dorothy's memory and the old wheeled bear was sold with other possessions from the deceased estate. Fortunately for the old bear, he landed on his wheels and found a very comfortable home not far from Kew.

THE BEAR ESSENTIALS — THE ROGERS FAMILY BEAR

DATE OF BIRTH:
1920 made in Germany by Schuco

HEIGHT:
20 in or 51 cm long
and 16 in or 41 cm high

FUR TYPE:
Short golden colour bristle mohair,
worn condition

FILLING:
Metal rod skeleton padded firmly
with excelsior/wood-wool

EYES AND EARS:
Original clear glass eyes;
ears rounded, set high
between a horizontal seam
on top of head

HEAD CHARACTERISTICS:
Head originally articulated;
neck joint now stitched together
and covered with red felt collar;
prominent snout; centre seam
runs vertically between ears
and down to nose;
short horizontal dart
just above eyes

BODY CHARACTERISTICS:
Metal rod skeleton; straight legs,
three claws on each foot,
wooden wheels supported
by round metal rods;
faint lettering on wheels
marked "Floresta" a trade name
used by Scheyer & Co. (Schuco);
length of chain attached
to front metal rod enabled bear
to be pulled along; short stumpy tail;
growl box, pull chain type
set into centre of back,
still in operation.

DISTINGUISHING FEATURES:
Blue felt saddle handstitched
onto bear's back to cover worn areas,
red felt collar added to strengthen
neck joint.

—RUDOLPH AND HENRIETTA—

Courtesy of Judy and John Sparrow, The Bear Museum, Petersfield, Hants, England.

RUDOLPH AND Henrietta are two beautiful old Steiff teddy bears made in Germany circa 1905. Both bears are great favourites of their owner Judy Sparrow.

By 1984, Judy's personal collection of teddies had expanded so rapidly that, together with her husband John, she decided to turn her entire collection of bears into Britain's first public teddy bear museum.

Henrietta Bear (far right) was purchased from an elderly lady who had treasured the bear as a child and had made the white cotton petticoat and apron the bear still wears today. The much loved bear had been well cared for and was in excellent condition. She had a working voice box and featured a rare seam down the centre of her head, something only one in every seven bears manufactured by Steiff received. Judy fell in love with Henrietta and felt the bear would make an excellent exhibit for her Petersfield Bear Museum. So when Henrietta was auctioned in 1985, despite considerable nail biting and competitive bidding, Judy and John managed to purchase the bear for £2,000, a world record price for a teddy bear at the time.

Henrietta's companion, Rudolph, is also in excellent condition for a bear circa 1905 but he has obviously not led the privileged life of Henrietta. When Judy first examined Rudolph she noticed that his voice box was not working and a strange rattling sound emanated from within his body. Carefully unpicking his seams Judy found that his voice box bellows had been completely split in two by an airgun pellet which was still lodged inside. Although there was only a very small hole on the outside of the bear's fur, it was obvious that poor Rudolph had, at some stage, been shot by a naughty child with an airgun.

Once Rudolph's surgery was completed he was also dressed in antique baby clothes. He now sits alongside the aristocratic Henrietta and bores her with tales of his bravery.

THE BEAR ESSENTIALS — RUDOLPH AND HENRIETTA

DATE OF BIRTH:
Both circa 1905 Steiff bears
made in Germany

HEIGHT:
20 in or 51 cm

FUR TYPE:
Henrietta has gold mohair
in very good condition,
Rudolph has dark gold mohair
in good condition,

FILLING:
Excelsior/wood-wool

EYES AND EARS:
Both have boot-button eyes

HEAD CHARACTERISTICS:
Both have shaved muzzle
cup-shaped ears; black silk nose,
vertically stitched;
Henrietta has a rare centre
head seam

BODY CHARACTERISTICS:
Both have hump on back;
very long arms and shaped legs
with narrow ankles and large feet

DISTINGUISHING FEATURES:
Henrietta has rare centre head seam,
Rudolph's growl box was spliced
in two by pellet from an airgun

–Sister Caedmon's Bear–

Public Collection. Courtesy of the Museum of the City of New York, New York, the United States.

SISTER CAEDMON'S teddy bear is a resident at the Museum of the City of New York, in the United States. For many years the museum has been collecting interesting toys which belonged to New York residents and this little bear has a touching history.

Elizabeth Wagner was given her teddy in 1914 on her second birthday. The Wagner family travelled constantly during Elizabeth's early years and her teddy bear was a constant companion who became a source of security for the little girl.

In 1914 Elizabeth's father was stationed on Governor's Island, a small island off Manhattan. Not long after the family moved again, this time to the Panama Canal area. However they had to return to the United States when the First World War broke out. Once the war was over the family was on the move again, this time setting sail for France. Young Elizabeth was told she could take only one toy on board. As she later recalled "At that tender age I thought the toy should be a doll, although I was never a doll person, so teddy had to make the trip in the hold, in spite of my fervent pleas to get him".

When teddy and Elizabeth were finally reunited at the end of the trip he never left her side. He even accompanied Elizabeth on a school camping trip where, while singing campfire songs, he sat a little too close to the camp fire and burnt his feet. His paws were repaired with leather and, fortunately, teddy seemed none the worse for his fiery adventure.

When she was 15 years old Elizabeth was stricken with poliomyelitis and hospitalised for 13 months. Fortunately she recovered and was later able to return to high school where she graduated valedictorian and went on to the William and Mary College. At the age of 24 Elizabeth joined the Episcopal order and took the name of Sister Caedmon. Teddy followed her there and stayed with her as she progressed into important administrative positions.

Elizabeth as a child with her teddy bear and other toys

In 1981, when Sister Caedmon was 69 years old, she donated her beloved bear to the Museum of the City of New York. He had been her friend and talisman for many years and she wished to ensure he would have a loving home in the future. A wise decision, for today this faithful and well-travelled teddy bear is a treasured member of the toy collection.

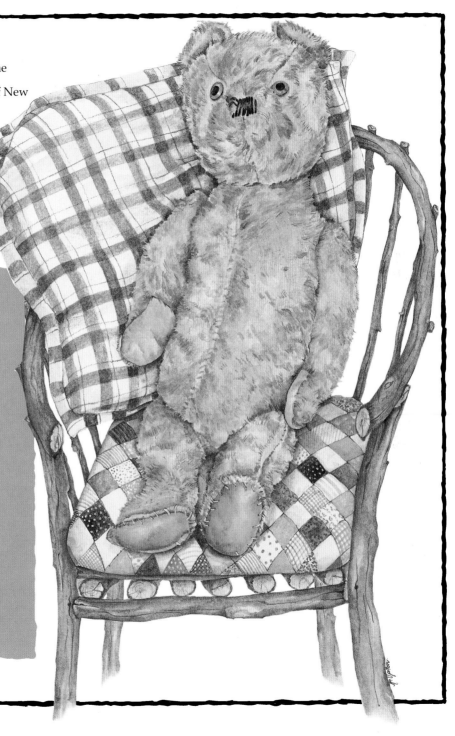

THE BEAR ESSENTIALS — SISTER CAEDMON'S BEAR

DATE OF BIRTH:
1914

HEIGHT:
16 in or 40 cm

FUR TYPE:
Golden coloured mohair, fair condition

FILLING:
Excelsior/wood-wool

EYES AND EARS:
Amber glass eyes, original;
ears set across side seam on head

HEAD CHARACTERISTICS:
Nose, black silk, vertically stitched; no mouth stitching;
rounded head

BODY CHARACTERISTICS:
Short curved arms; paw pads replaced;
foot pads replaced with leather

DISTINGUISHING FEATURES:
No mouth stitching; burnt areas on feet replaced
with brown leather

-THE STEIFF MUSEUM-

Courtesy of Margarete Steiff GmbH, Giengen (Brenz), Germany.

THE MOST-famous teddy bear manufacturer, the Steiff toy company, was founded by Margarete Steiff in 1880. This innovative German company played a leading role in the development of the teddy bear and today Steiff teddies are the most coveted of bears.

The founder of the company, Margarete Steiff, was stricken with poliomyelitis as a child and, as a result of the illness, was confined to a wheelchair. Fortunately she was blessed with a vibrant

enthusiasm for life and was also a keen businesswoman.

She was the first in her village of Giengen to own a sewing machine and, by placing the machine back to front, she overcame the weakness in her right hand to begin work making felt underskirts. From the remnants of felt she made small toys which proved very popular, especially a felt elephant. Her range of toys increased steadily year by year and, with the help of her family, Steiff rapidly became a successful company.

In the early 1900s the craze for teddy bears swept the world. Steiff was quick to seize the initiative and was soon manufacturing handsome teddy bears that were

exported all over the world. From 1905 every bear which left the factory had the Steiff toy company's famous trademark — a button in ear — which was a small metal button affixed to the toy's left ear.

Renowned for its creativity and quality, Steiff retained samples of almost every toy it made. This treasure trove of toy samples narrowly escaped being lost at the end of the Second World War when Allied troops occupied Germany. Such goods were typically seized as reparations but a loyal Steiff employee arranged for numerous crates of the precious toy samples to be hidden and they escaped confiscation.

This extensive collection of sample toys comprises the backbone of the Steiff Museum, which is situated alongside the Steiff factory in picturesque Giengen, Germany. The vast collection of Steiff toys is arranged in chronological order and begins with Margarete Steiff's first felt elephant and ranges through to present day production.

The variety and quality of the beautiful Steiff toys on display at the museum is quite staggering. Margarete Steiff died in 1909 but the Steiff toy company carries on manufacturing to her high standards, recalling Margarete's famous motto "Only the best is good enough for our children".

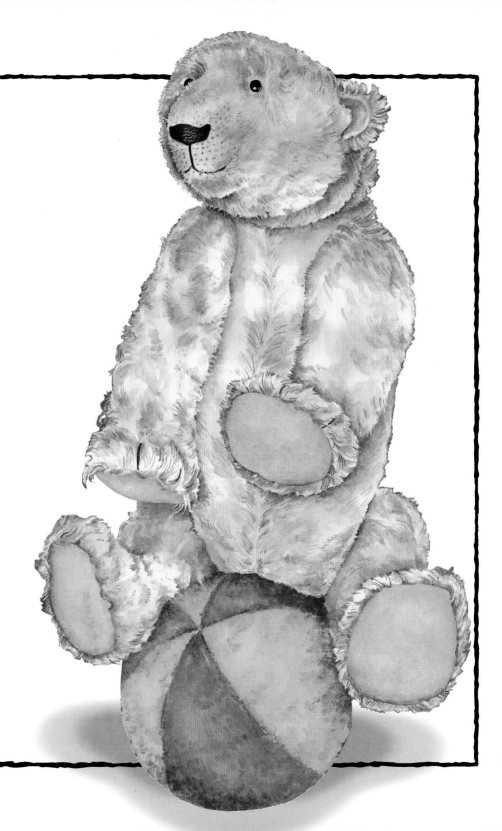

THE BEAR ESSENTIALS
– POLAR BEAR

DATE OF BIRTH:
Circa early 1900s

FUR TYPE::
White bristle mohair

EYES AND EARS:
Black boot-button eyes

**HEAD
CHARACTERISTICS:**
Shaved muzzle; head attached by swivel
ball-jointed mechanism

BODY CHARACTERISTICS:
Moveable limbs; enormous pink
felt paws

**DISTINGUISHING
FEATURES**
Constructed with a jointed head and
moveable limbs allowing it to be
moved in a realistic fashion

—The Stratford-upon-Avon Bears—

Public Collection. Courtesy of the Teddy Bear Museum, Stratford-upon-Avon, Warwickshire, England.

IN WILLIAM Shakespeare's day the wonderful old Elizabethan building which presently houses the Teddy Bear Museum in Stratford-upon-Avon was a farmhouse. Nowadays, beneath the original oak beams of the historic building, a large collection of teddy bears is cleverly displayed in miniature room settings. These settings include a library for scholarly bears and a music room where teddies, old and new, gather around the piano for a sing-song.

The museum is home to many distinguished bears, who were once owned by famous people. For example, Percy was once owned by the Marquess of Bath who organised a successful teddy bears' picnic which was held at historic Longleat. Another bear, Prince of Love, was once owned by romantic novelist Barbara Cartland. Ms Cartland bedecked the bear from head to foot in flamboyant faux jewels and was even inspired to write him the following poem.

I am a special teddy bear
I am particular what I wear
My diamonds gleam like stars above
As really I am the Prince of Love

Sitting near the celebrity corner are two old friends from the early 1900s sharing a bunch of flowers. The larger bear was made by the famous Steiff company in 1903 — during the early days of teddy bear production. It was a time of experimentation for the company and the bear's unusually large, flat ears are set wide apart on the sides of his head. This rare and beautiful bear is in excellent condition with luxurious wavy fur, narrow ankles and fine long feet. Subsequent design changes resulted in Steiff bears having standard cup-shaped ears which were set closer together. His companion, dressed in a red knitted suit, was made in 1906 and also hails from the Steiff company. He features the famous Steiff trademark, a metal button in ear (see page 110). This little bear was purchased for £520 in 1987, from Sotheby's auction house, by Gyles and Michele Brandreth. They fell in love with his cheeky appearance and knew he would be a wonderful addition to their museum. The little bear's winsome good looks have been captured on film and he is featured on the front cover of the museum's catalogue.

Sadly, teddy bears did not exist in Shakespeare's day for there can be no doubt that if they had he would have been the first to write of their charms.

THE BEAR ESSENTIALS —

LARGE BEAR HOLDING FLOWERS

DATE OF BIRTH:
1903 Steiff bear made in Germany

HEIGHT:
25 in or 65 cm

FUR TYPE:
Long wavy golden coloured mohair

FILLING:
Excelsior/wood-wool

EYES AND EARS:
Large, black, boot-button type eyes, original; large flat ears set well apart on head

HEAD CHARACTERISTICS:
Broad head; pointed muzzle with original nose and mouth features intact stitched in light tan thread with vertical stitches

BODY CHARACTERISTICS:
Prominent hump on back; extremely long curved arms and shaped legs with very narrow ankles; long feet with original beige felt on all paws, worn in places on feet to reveal red felt lining material; claws stitched in light tan thread

DISTINGUISHING FEATURES:
Unusual wide head design with large flat ears; stuffing displaced in top part of arms, usually the result of a child holding the toy at this point; felt on feet worn, repaired with small beige stitches

BEAR IN RED KNITTED SUIT

DATE OF BIRTH:
1906 Steiff bear made in Germany

HEIGHT:
13 in or 33 cm

FUR TYPE:
Light golden coloured mohair, good condition

FILLING:
Excelsior/wood-wool

EYES AND EARS:
Small, boot-button eyes original; small cupped ears with edges caught into side seams

HEAD CHARACTERISTICS:
Fairly broad head and pointed shaved muzzle; nose stitched horizontally with dark brown thread, enclosed stitch around lower edges

BODY CHARACTERISTICS:
Hump on back; well made small bear with long arms and large feet; claws stitched in dark brown thread and all felt pads replaced

DISTINGUISHING FEATURES:
Steiff trademark metal button in ear; golden coloured fur in good condition; very cheeky appearance in knitted red suit

—SUE PEARSON BEARS—

Courtesy of Sue Pearson, Brighton, England.

SUE PEARSON'S Antique Doll and Teddy Bear shop in Brighton, England is a collector's haven. There is an abundance of bears for arctophiles to admire and her window displays are a veritable feast of charming old bears. Sue travels extensively to ensure a constant supply of appealing toys for her shop and has written several books on the subject.

Teddy bear collectors are always keen to acquire at least some knowledge of a bear's history and the small Steiff bear tucked up in his wooden cot was fortunate enough to be in possession of an old family photograph which showed his original owner. In the picture she wore a large white bow in her hair and stood shyly clutching the bear to her side.

On a recent trip to Sue's shop Goodnight was discovered, a bear made by the Chad Valley Hygienic Toy Company in 1928. He had been left at the shop by an elderly woman from Sussex who told Sue the bear had belonged to her late sister. Since there were no children in her family to pass him to, she hoped Sue could find a caring home for him. Goodnight was a well equipped bear. He was still wearing his original pink dressing gown and had a sponge and a small hot water-bottle tied to his waist. A linen wash bag which had been carefully embroidered with the words GOOD NIGHT hung around his neck.

Teddy bears work their magic by night as they comfort their owners to sleep. Soft, and familiar, bears are the ultimate protectors against disorder and things that go bump in the night. Most bears spend a lifetime in the bedroom, so it comes as no surprise that many old teddies arrive for sale wearing a bizarre assortment of nightdresses and pyjamas.

Both Sue's bears obviously look forward to a good eight hours sleep. Sleep tight Goodnight.

THE BEAR ESSENTIALS – GOODNIGHT

DATE OF BIRTH:
1928 made in England by the Chad Valley Hygienic Toy Company

HEIGHT:
15 in or 38 cm

FUR TYPE:
Golden coloured mohair plush, worn in places

FILLING:
Excelsior/wood-wool

EYES AND EARS:
Large dome-shaped amber glass eyes; large flat ears, set well apart on head with inner edge of ear set into seam

HEAD CHARACTERISTICS:
Broad head, stuffing displaced in muzzle; nose possibly restitched

BODY CHARACTERISTICS:
Fairly short straight arms; all paw pads repaired with brown felt, five widely spaced claws on each foot

DISTINGUISHING FEATURES:
Crease above nose where stuffing is displaced; arrived wearing a dressing gown of pink cotton printed fabric with a Japanese design, fashionable during the 1920s; original Chad Valley label re-sewn to his foot

—TED BEAR—

Private Collection. Courtesy of Heather and family, Melbourne, Victoria, Australia.

TED BEAR was made in 1909 and has enjoyed a long and adventurous life. He was a farewell gift to a young couple, Jeannie and Edward McKee, who were leaving their beloved Kilmacolm, Scotland for a new life in Australia. As the couple bade a sad farewell to family and friends before embarking on their long sea journey, Jeannie was filled with trepidation.

The voyage to Australia via the East was a long, often hazardous trip. Jeannie was also expecting their first child and her concerns about making the journey deepened when Edward became seriously ill from a fever. The couple reached Sydney and, in September 1911, Jeannie gave birth to a fine baby boy whom they named Edward. Sadly, five months later, the baby's father Edward McKee passed away.

Jeannie and baby Edward were now alone in Australia and Jeannie decided to sail

home to Scotland to be with her family. She packed their few treasured possessions for the long journey and, naturally, Ted Bear accompanied them.

A few years later Jeannie returned to Australia. She sailed on the Orsova with young Edward, then aged two, and the world travelling Ted Bear.

This time Jeannie enjoyed the long voyage. She joined in the entertainments on board and entered Edward into a baby contest held on the ship. Handsome little Edward took first prize and Jeannie's descendants still have the engraved silver napkin holder awarded as his prize.

Jeannie made many friends on the journey, in particular with a young pianist from the ship's orchestra named Charles Carter. As the ship neared Sydney, Jeannie and Charles parted reluctantly and Jeannie made her way to Melbourne to stay with relatives. However Charles had fallen in love and a few months later he returned to Melbourne to search for Jeannie. Eventually he found her. The happy couple were married and set up home together for Edward junior and Ted Bear.

Ted Bear is a treasured and much loved heirloom and has remained with his original family for over three generations.

Right: Jeannie with Edward Jr, Ted's owner (1915)
Below: Jeannie's granddaughter Heather, Ted's current owner (circa 1930s)

He presently lives with Heather, Jeannie's granddaughter, who is now a grandmother herself and who intends Ted to be passed down to her grandchildren. Meanwhile, Ted Bear spends a comfortable retirement in his own chair remembering his seafaring days.

THE BEAR ESSENTIALS — TED BEAR

DATE OF BIRTH:
1909 made in England

HEIGHT:
30 in or 76 cm

FUR TYPE:
Wavy golden coloured mohair, good condition

FILLING:
Excelsior/wood-wool

EYES AND EARS:
Large glass eyes, not original; ears set across side seams on head

HEAD CHARACTERISTICS:
Large head; pronounced shaved snout; repaired mouth; nose, vertically stitched, original

BODY CHARACTERISTICS:
Quality bear in the style of Alpha Farnell; hump on back; long arms with slight curve; legs well defined with large cardboard lined feet; paw and foot pads all replaced with cotton twill (originally beige felt); tip up growl box, still in operation

DISTINGUISHING FEATURES:
Hand stitched smile in black twill using a blanket stitch

117

—TREASURE BEAR—

Private Collection. Courtesy of Nancy, Victoria, Australia.

NANCY, ONE of nine children, was born in South Gippsland, Victoria, Australia. Soon after the birth of the youngest child Nancy's father abandoned the family and sold all their possessions, including the children's toys. Despite financial hardships, Nancy's mother ensured her five sons and four daughters became a close, loving family.

Many years later Nancy became a teddy bear collector. Most of her bears were so old and bedraggled they had simply been discarded but under Nancy's tender care they again blossomed into desirable characters.

Treasure, an old teddy from the 1930s, is a perfect example of such a transformation. Years ago, while at a charity sale, Nancy watched as some old toy pedal cars were auctioned. Prices were high and many of the cars were purchased by a local antique dealer. A few weeks later

Nancy happened to visit the dealer and noticed a trailer load of rubbish parked outside his shop. As she approached she saw a lumpy bear-shaped object perched on top of the trash and, after requesting a closer look, Nancy was told by the dealer she would be disappointed as it was just an old bear in hopeless condition. The bear had lost both eyes as well as an arm, it was squashed almost flat and its fur was covered with red paint to which bits of newspaper had stuck. The dealer told Nancy he had found the old teddy while repairing a pedal car which seemed unable to turn. Fearing the mechanism was at fault he had turned the car upside down to find the old bear jammed beneath the steering rod.

Despite the teddy's pitiful condition Nancy offered the surprised dealer 50 cents and took the bear home. There she worked painstakingly on his stained coat with eucalyptus oil and a doctor's scalpel. Slowly the hardened paint was removed to reveal patchy golden coloured fur and an old Joy Toys label was discovered on the bear's right foot. It was love at first sight for Nancy and, because of the bear's association with trash, she cleverly named him Treasure.

Sitting next to Treasure in the car is Barnaby, a bear with sad woollen eyes who emigrated from the United States to Australia during the early 1900s. The little bear standing alongside the car in a sailor suit was named American Express by Nancy, simply because she "never leaves home without him". American Express and Barnaby were both left to Nancy by a close friend.

It must be said that Nancy's bears have excellent taste as they appear to have chosen Nancy almost as surely as she has chosen them. A loving mother of eight and grandmother of eighteen, Nancy works tirelessly for charity. Indeed, Nancy could be described as something of a treasure herself.

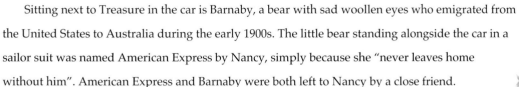

THE BEAR ESSENTIALS — TREASURE

DATE OF BIRTH:
Circa 1930 made in Australia by Joy Toys

HEIGHT:
17 in or 43 cm

FUR TYPE:
Golden coloured mohair, very worn

FILLING:
Excelsior/wood-wool

EYES AND EARS:
Eyes missing; rounded ears with inner edge set in facial seams

HEAD CHARACTERISTICS:
Defined muzzle; nose stitched in black silk with elongated stitch on either side; mouth missing; articulated head (later bears made by Joy Toys had stiff necks)

BODY CHARACTERISTICS:
Lozenge-shaped body; small hump on back; upturned paws; little shaping to feet; Joy Toys label on right foot

DISTINGUISHING FEATURES:
Traces of red and green paint on fur; Treasure has no eyes, he is missing a right arm and is a little squashed from many years beneath the pedal car

—WHITIE—

WHITIE, an old bear from 1906, lives in the Bethnal Green Museum of Childhood in London. He spends many hours gazing thoughtfully into space with the kind of expression only a wise old bear can achieve.

Whitie was donated to the museum in 1983 by Mrs Edwards but he originally belonged to Jess Fraser, who was born in 1905. Jess named her bear Whitie and she obviously loved him dearly as he is patched all over and his well worn pads have been carefully repaired with new claw stitches which extend to both sides of his paws. When Whitie arrived at the museum he still wore original baby clothes from the early 1900s. His pale blue woollen dress had been carefully embroidered with dark blue silk and he wore a linen petticoat, cream cotton knickers and a knitted vest. Whitie's outfit also consisted of mercerised cotton

THE BEAR ESSENTIALS — WHITIE BEAR

DATE OF BIRTH:
1905 probably made in Germany

HEIGHT:
20 in or 51 cm

FUR TYPE:
Long golden coloured mohair, patchy.

FILLING:
Excelsior/wood-wool.

EYES AND EARS:
Black metal eyes; large ears

HEAD CHARACTERISTICS:
Prominent snout; repairs on muzzle;
original vertically stitched nose

BODY CHARACTERISTICS:
Quality toy of the period and typical
of early teddy bear design;
prominent snout; humped back;
long curved arms; paw pads not original,
repaired with cream cotton

DISTINGUISHING FEATURES:
Unusual repair work on paws of bear;
claws have been stitched both inner
and outer sides of paws

socks and soft leather shoes tied with blue ribbon.

All the teddy bears in the museum are constantly rearranged to provide new and interesting displays but Whitie and the Sailor Bear are usually seated together because they complement each other so perfectly. Sailor Bear, a handsome teddy made in Germany in 1911, is dressed as a First World War sailor and his white cotton shirt was carefully hand-sewn for him many years ago by the nuns of Malta.

With such an impressive uniform it is hard to believe Sailor Bear can't capture his partner's attention, however it seems Whitie's thoughts are elsewhere.

—Winnie-the-Pooh—

Public Collection. Courtesy of The Collection of the Central Children's Room, Donnell Library Center, The New York Public Library, New York, United States.

Christopher Robin feeds Winnie-the-Pooh biscuits, (circa 1928)

NO BOOK about teddy bears would be complete without mention of Winnie-the-Pooh, the famous bear immortalised by A.A. Milne in his book *Winnie-the-Pooh* , written in the 1920s. The story of "the bear of little brain" and his young owner, Christopher Robin, has captivated children and their parents for generations.

Winnie-the-Pooh was purchased by the Milnes in 1921 from Harrods department store in London for their son Christopher Robin's first birthday. Known initially as Bear or Teddy he obtained his famous name after Christopher Robin visited an American black bear in the London Zoo named Winnie and combined this name with that of a swan he knew called Pooh. Christopher Robin was an only child and sometimes felt a little lonely but Winnie-the-Pooh became his favourite companion and the two were inseparable.

The Milnes had a farm in Cotchford, Sussex and Ashdown Forest was nearby. Christopher Robin would often play in the forest inside his favourite walnut tree which had a large hollow, just big enough for himself and Pooh.

Milne was inspired to write his famous stories after overhearing young Christopher Robin and Winnie-the-Pooh as they chatted together. Other characters from Christopher Robin's toy box soon appeared in the books and each was given an easily identifiable personality.

Christopher Robin was cast as the capable child hero. The bear, Winnie-the-Pooh, managed to bluff his way through the problems of life while squeaky Piglet, given to Christopher Robin by a neighbour, was never far behind. Eeyore, the donkey, had a sad drooping neck and so was a natural for a gloomy disposition. Tigger, Kanga and Roo were selected after another visit to the Harrods toy department in search of new characters. Tigger's bouncy personality was based on an energetic spaniel dog once owned by the family, while Owl and Rabbit simply sprang from Milne's imagination. When the characters were combined with the remarkable illustrative talent of E.H. Shepard, the magic was complete. Shepard went to great pains to capture the appeal of the toys and made numerous sketches of them with Christopher Robin in Ashdown Forest. Shepard admitted to occasionally using his son's bear, Growler, as a model. Growler, a rather plump bear, was described by Shepard as "a magnificent bear. I have never seen his like".

As for Winnie-the-Pooh, Piglet, Eeyore, Tigger and Kanga (little Roo was lost in an apple orchard during the 1930s), the famous toys made several trips back and forth to the United States to promote the books, until Milne decided they should become American citizens.

Winnie-the-Pooh, Piglet, Eeyore, Tigger and Kanga have never been restored as it was Milne's wish that the toys should always appear as if a child has just finished playing with them. The toys range in size from Eeyore, who is 25 in or 64 cm, to Piglet, who is a a mere 4 in or 11 cm.

The famous toys now sit comfortably in the Children's Room of the New York Public Library, protected in a glass case. For the picture and for old time's sake we put Pooh and Piglet back to dream in Ashdown Forest.

(With grateful acknowledgement to Ann Thwaite,
author of *A.A. Milne: His Life* and *The Brilliant Career of Winnie-the-Pooh*.)

THE BEAR ESSENTIALS — WINNIE-THE-POOH

DATE OF BIRTH:
1921 made in England,
probably by Alfa Farnell

HEIGHT:
18 in or 46 cm

FUR TYPE:
Wavy golden coloured mohair,
fair condition

FILLING:
Kapok

EYES AND EARS:
Large amber glass eyes;
large ears which appear
a little lopsided

HEAD CHARACTERISTICS:
Clipped muzzle;
nose and mouth embroidered
with brown silk

BODY CHARACTERISTICS:
Long arms; shaped legs
with slim ankles and large feet;
paw and foot pads repaired
many times, foot pads patched
and stitched all over

DISTINGUISHING FEATURES:
There can only
be one Pooh

—THE WORLAND BEARS—

Private Collection. Courtesy of David Worland,
Sydney, New South Wales, Australia.

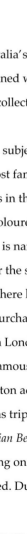

DAVID WORLAND has been aptly dubbed "Australia's First Man of Teddies". His enthusiasm for the subject, combined with his generosity in sharing his extensive knowledge and bear collection, make him an excellent ambassador for bear enthusiasts.

David's unflagging interest in his subject has led him to track down the most famous and interesting teddy bears in the world. The large cinnamon coloured Steiff teddy bear on the left is named Brompton after the street where he was purchased — the Old Brompton Road in London where Christie's, the famous auction house, is situated. Brompton accompanies David on his many overseas trips and 'writes' a column for *Australian Bear Facts Review* magazine, reporting on the bear-related events he has attended. During one of Brompton's

David's father, Gerald A. Worland, as a baby (1910) with an early Steiff teddy bear

memorable journeys across the Atlantic he flew Concorde and sat beside the late British character actor, Robert Morley. Morley, renowned for his dry sense of humour, made no comment when seated alongside the large teddy bear. As Brompton and Morley were both served delicious smoked salmon and champagne, Morley's larger than life personality and appetite assisted the bear with his dinner. Morley adored eating and once said he could never understand people who weighed themselves, as one may as well measure the length of one's hair. Morley found the bear an admirable travelling companion, far better than most.

Loring, the small bear in a safari suit, represents an amazing piece of teddy bear history. In 1910 President Roosevelt returned from a safari in British East Africa and a celebratory dinner was held in New York for all those who had accompanied him on the trip. Each guest found a small Steiff teddy bear at their place setting as a token of thanks. Loring is the only known surviving teddy from the occasion. Given to J. Alden Loring, a young Smithsonian naturalist, the bear was treasured by several generations of the Loring family.

It would be understandable if magnificent bears such as these were locked away behind glass, however, the Worland bears are cuddled, patted and taken to exciting teddy bear events all around the world. What more could any bear ask for?

THE BEAR ESSENTIALS —

BROMPTON	LORING
DATE OF BIRTH: 1907 Steiff bear made in Germany	**DATE OF BIRTH:** 1910 Steiff bear made in Germany
HEIGHT: 24 in or 61 cm	**HEIGHT:** 12 in or 31 cm
FUR TYPE: Cinnamon coloured mohair fur, excellent condition	**FUR TYPE:** Light golden coloured mohair, worn in places
FILLING: Excelsior/wood-wool	**FILLING:** Excelsior/wood-wool
EYES AND EARS: Black, button type eyes; original, well spaced ears	**EYES AND EARS:** Original boot-button type eyes; well spaced ears; Steiff button in ear
HEAD CHARACTERISTICS: Shaved snout and stern expression	**HEAD CHARACTERISTICS:** Shaved snout; original nose stitching; fur a little worn giving the appearance of a ruff around bear's face
BODY CHARACTERISTICS: Long limbs, typical of Steiff bears of the period	**BODY CHARACTERISTICS:** Long limbs; original paw stitching
DISTINGUISHING FEATURES: Brompton usually wears a red Teddy Roosevelt campaign scarf	**DISTINGUISHING FEATURES:** Loring has a custom-made safari suit to commemorate President Roosevelt's African expedition of 1910 with boots to protect his slightly worn feet, Loring wears his prestigious Show Favourite award from the 1991 Festival of Steiff

—THE WORTHING BEARS—

Public Collection. The Worthing Museum and Art Gallery, Worthing, England.

2OO YEARS AGO Worthing was a small fishing hamlet on the English coast. During the 1700s the medical profession began to recommend the curative powers of bracing sea air and doctors advised bathing in and even drinking sea water. In 1798 a member of the royal family, Princess Amelia, visited Worthing to convalesce. Well-to-do health enthusiasts were quick to follow in her footsteps and, almost overnight, Worthing became a fashionable resort.

Nowadays things are a little quieter and the Worthing Museum and Art Gallery, situated in Chapel Street, houses an interesting toy collection with some very appealing teddy bears, most of whom have been donated by residents of the town.

Teddy James was made in England and dates from 1922. This well dressed bear once belonged to Miss Rosemary James who made all his clothes, paying such attention to detail that she even lined his corduroy jacket with contrasting fabric. Teddy James has extraordinarily large orange eyes and fixes a hard stare at his companion, a small bear who dates from 1910.

Sitting on the sand with his windmill and bucket, is a little bear from 1907. He is believed to be a Steiff bear but has lost the trademark metal button in ear (see page 110). As a result of spending many afternoons sitting on the beach with his original owner, his fur has faded to an unusual olive brown colour.

Nowadays he looks a little melancholy, but when the sun comes out and the sea breeze picks up enough to spin his windmill everything changes. All the bears were donated to the Worthing Museum.

THE BEAR ESSENTIALS – WINDMILL BEAR

DATE OF BIRTH:
1907 made in Germany, probably by Steiff

HEIGHT:
10 in or 26 cm

FUR TYPE:
Olive brown mohair plush, worn in places

FILLING:
Excelsior/wood-wool

EYES AND EARS:
Black, round boot-button eyes, original; cup-shaped ears set across head seams

HEAD CHARACTERISTICS:
Pronounced, clipped muzzle; brown silk nose, original

BODY CHARACTERISTICS:
Small hump on bear's back; very long arms and shaped legs with original felt paws and pads

DISTINGUISHING FEATURES:
Unusual olive brown fur; sad, but appealing expression

TEDDY JAMES

DATE OF BIRTH:
1922 made in England

HEIGHT:
15 in or 40 cm

EYES AND EARS:
Extremely large yellow/orange eyes

BODY CHARACTERISTICS:
Original cotton twill pads with four claws on his paws and five on his feet

DISTINGUISHING FEATURES:
He wears light tan velvet trousers and beret, a mustard coloured corduroy jacket lined with spotted fabric and a shirt and tie, all believed to have been made by his owner, Rosemary James

—Yootha's Bear—

Public Collection. Courtesy of The Brighton Borough Council, Administrators for the Rottingdean Toy Museum, Sussex, England.

THIS OLD bear and his toy clown companion live at the Rottingdean Toy Museum. Both toys once belonged to the founder of the museum, Yootha Rose, who was an accomplished artist and toymaker during the 1920s.

Although she lived most of her life in England, Yootha Rose was born in Australia in 1899, when her father, a singer, was touring Australia with the Nellie Melba Company. Her theatrical parents named her Yootha, an Aboriginal word meaning bringer of luck.

Yootha Rose was a respected artist. Her skills extended to stage and costume design but she is mainly remembered for her highly original toymaking. Yootha Rose was described as the "Royal Toymaker" because the Royal family were keen patrons of her colourful wooden toys. Queen Mary commissioned a miniature roundabout during the early 1950s for the young Prince Charles, and thereafter Yootha designed many charming toys for the royal nursery. One of her last commissions was a miniature zoo, created in 1978, for Princess Anne's son Peter Phillips. Nowadays, Yootha's colourful toys are valuable collector items.

Yootha's bear, circa 1906, has lost much of his wood-wool filling and has a delightfully saggy and relaxed appearance. He displays all the typical features of early teddy bears, including a prominent humped back and a long snout with just a thread or two of his original stitched nose remaining. The old bear's large feet have been extravagantly repaired with thick red velvet, possibly a remnant of an old stage curtain from one of Yootha's theatrical projects.

Alongside Yootha's bear is his companion, a toy clown, who is part of a set called The Humpty Dumpty Circus which was made in 1903 by Albert Schoenhut in the United States. Beautifully fashioned in wood, the characters include clowns, elephants and horses, all brightly painted and articulated. The set would certainly have appealed to Yootha, who clearly understood what a child requires of a toy.

Yootha's old bear relaxes in a corner of the museum and wisely casts his one remaining boot-button eye down at the painted clown.

THE BEAR ESSENTIALS — YOOTHA'S BEAR

DATE OF BIRTH:
1906 probably made in Germany

HEIGHT:
22 in or 56 cm

FUR TYPE:
Golden coloured mohair,
very worn condition

FILLING:
Excelsior/wood-wool

EYES AND EARS:
One original boot-button eye,
large ears set across facial seams

HEAD CHARACTERISTICS:
Wide head, prominent snout,
black stitching on nose worn

BODY CHARACTERISTICS:
Prominent humped back;
broad upper body with long arms
and legs; three claws on each paw

DISTINGUISHING FEATURES:
Stuffing badly displaced in body
giving bear saggy appearance;
one eye is missing;
all paws have been replaced
with red/tan velvet

129

DEDICATION

To my parents
for all their love
and for giving me
my first teddy bear.

To Mark,
for his gentle
encouragement, who
owns the strangest
bear in the land.

To Christian,
for his outrageous sense
of humour, who always
chose his own bear.

And to Paul, my best friend
who waited and waited and waited.
Love forever.

And to all the people who generously shared their bears and their time
in order for me to record these fascinating histories and portraits.

ACKNOWLEDGMENTS

I would sincerely like to thank all the HarperCollins team, particularly Alison Mahoney for her enthusiasm and expertise, Elissa Grierson for her sympathetic editing and Cathy Campbell and Neil Carlyle for their insightful design, in bringing this book to life.

My grateful thanks to all the generous people who assisted with this book, including:

Jan Edwards for Aged Bear

The ever generous Judy and John Sparrow at the Petersfield Bear Museum, England for Albert, Clown Bear, Rudolph, Henrietta and Plummy — Hurrah for Albert!

Ian Pout and staff at Teddy Bears of Witney, England for Alfonzo

Mary Lewis and curatorial staff at the State Library of Victoria, Australia for the Bear and Batman's Doll

Peter and sons for Bill Bear

The curatorial staff at the Spielzeugmuseum, Germany for the Bridal Bears

All the excellent curatorial staff at the Bethnal Green Museum of Childhood, England for the Cattley Family Toys, Little Tommy Tittlemouse and Whitie

National Trust of Tasmania, Australia, and, in particular, Joan Green for the Clarendon Bears, grateful thanks also to Julie Rockliff and Michael Bell

National Trust of Victoria, Australia and Beth Dodgson for Como Bear, thanks also to Edna's nieces, Wilma and Lorna

The invincible Alison for Ded Ted

Ian Gardner and curatorial staff at the Museum of Childhood, Scotland for the Edinburgh Bears

Hilary Moles for Elsie's Bear

Des and Monica Carpenter at the Cotswold Teddy Bear Museum, Cotswolds, England for Fire Guard Bear, Fritz and Horatio, many thanks also to Wendy and Colin Lewis

Forby's best friend, thank you

Alan and Kathleen for Gertrude's Bear

Gillian Knight for Gillian's Bear

Diana Henderson at the Arundel Toy & Military Museum, England for the Good-time Ted and Friends

Frank for Growl, and many thanks to Betty Roberts

All the 'little' Harveys for Hatbox

Margaret Munday-Whitaker at the Lilliput Antique Doll & Toy Museum, Isle of Wight, England for Hilda's Bear

Jan Booth for Jan's Teddy

Joan Cockrill for Jessica Bear, and a bear hug to Pauline and David and the menagerie

Jane Hirschowitz and the curatorial staff at the Museum of the City of New York for Johnny Bear and Sister Caedmon's Bear

Jocie, Fiona and Sarah Adams for Jocie's Little Ted

To dear Janet and family for J.T. or Kim's teddy, with thanks also to 'Auntie Peg' and Gae

Little Red's only friend — keep wishing

Hamish MacGillivray and the curatorial staff at the London Toy & Model Museum, England for the London Toy Museum Bears

Melissa Wells for Melissa's Bear

Joy Lewis for Mister Bear

Robert Holden and the National Trust, New South Wales, Australia for the Merchants' House Bears

Pilchard's guardian

Kate and Sarah for Pillow

Veronica Sheppard and the curatorial staff at Pollocks Toy Museum, England for the Pollocks Toy Museum Bears

Kimberley and the curatorial staff at the Powerhouse Museum, Sydney, New South Wales, Australia for the Powerhouse Toys

To dear Richard for Richard's Rabbit

Richard Heathcote and the National Trust of Victoria, Australia for the Rippon Lea Bears

Robin Kelly for Robin's Bear

John and Betty Rogers for Dorothy Rogers Family Bear, with grateful thanks also to Robin Kelly

Margarete Steiff GmbH, Germany and Jan-Dirk Kohne for the Steiff Museum Bears

Gyles Brandreth and staff at Stratford-upon-Avon Bears, England for the excellent Alfonzo

Sue Pearson, Brighton, England for the Sue Pearson Bears

Heather and Graham for Ted

Nancy for Treasure and his pals

Edwin S. Holmgren and the staff at the New York Public Library for Winnie-the-Pooh, thanks to Ann Thwaite for her generous assistance

National Portrait Gallery in London for photo of Christopher Robin and Winnie-the-Pooh

Sally White and the curatorial staff at the Worthing Museum and Art Gallery, England for the Worthing Bears

David Worland for the wonderful Worland Bears

Marion Waller and curatorial staff at the Rottingdean Toy Museum, England for Yootha's Bear

Collection, Buda historic home and garden, Castlemaine, Victoria, Australia. Thanks to John Gowty.

Angus & Robertson

An imprint of HarperCollins*Publishers*, Australia

First published in Australia in 1995

HarperCollinsPublishers
25 Ryde Road, Pymble, Sydney NSW 2073, Australia
31 View Road, Glenfield, Auckland 10, New Zealand
77–85 Fulham Palace Road, London W6 8JB, United Kingdom
Hazelton Lanes, 55 Avenue Road, Suite 2900, Toronto, Ontario M5R 3L2
and 1995 Markham Road, Scarborough, Ontario M1B 5M8, Canada
10 East 53rd Street, New York NY 10032, USA

National Library of Australia Cataloguing-in-Publication data:

Upton, Rosalie
The secret lives of teddy bears: the stories of teddies
and the people who love them.

ISBN 0 207 18743 6.
1. Teddy bears – Pictorial works. 2. Teddy bears. I. Title.

6884.724

Printed in Hong Kong

9 8 7 6 5 4 3 2 1
99 98 97 96 95